Aging, Representation, and Thought

Aging, Representation, and Thought

Gestalt and Feature-Intensive Processing

Matthew J. Sharps

Transaction Publishers
New Brunswick (U.S.A.) and London (U.K.)

Library of Congress Catalog Number: 2002073209
ISBN: 0-7658-0152-3
Printed in the United States of America

Library of Congress Cataloging-in-Publication Data

Sharps, Matthew Joseph.
    Aging, representation, and thought : Gestalt and feature-intensive
    processing / Matthew Joseph Sharps.
        p. cm.
    Includes bibliographical references (p.   ) and index.
    ISBN 0-7658-0152-3 (alk. paper)
        1. Cognition in old age. 2. Human information processing. 3. Function-
alism (Psychology) 4. Gestalt psychology. I. Title.

BF724.85.C64 S53 2002
155.67'134—dc21

                                                                2002073209

For Jana

Contents

Acknowledgements   ix

Introduction and Plan of the Book   1

1. The Paradox of Human Intelligence   5

2. Minds through Time I: What Aging and
    Spatial Cognition Reveal about the Nature
    of Representation   17

3. Minds through Time II: What Aging and
    Nonspatial Cognition Reveal about the
    Nature of Representation   37

4. The Processing of Auditory Imagery   49

5. Gestalt and Feature-Intensive Processing:
    Toward a Unified Model of Human Information
    Processing   75

6. Bad Decisions, G/FI Processing, and Contextual
    Reasoning   107

    Epilogue   123

    Bibliography   125

    Index   137

List of Tables

Table 5.1— General Flowchart of Gestalt/Feature-
Intensive Processing

Acknowledgements

A great many people have contributed to the ideas set forth in this book, and to the book itself. I would like to thank all of the students whose ideas and hard work have contributed so much to this research over the years; in particular, and in rough chronological order from the earliest to the most recent, I would like to thank Dr. Lisa Maas, Laura Lake, Melissa Stegeman, Lisa Cook, David Diehl, Mike Tindall, Celeste Merryman, Heidi Barbis, Cheryl Manrique, Hart Broesel, Carla Wilson-Leff, Michael Bence, Janine Antonelli, Kiersten Handorf, Carol Shaible, Tammy Silva, Brandon Foster, Kevin Sears, Vince Corsaro, Brent Pollitt, Michelle Merrill, Sandra Mitchell, Ellen Woo, Shari Ahlberg, Amy Neff, Amy Boothby-Villegas, Terri Barber, and Justin Matthews. Particular thanks are due to Dr. Sandy Schulte (*née* Martin) and to Mike Nunes. Thanks also to Henry Placenti for his computer expertise in the preparation of this work. I would like to thank Professors Eugene S. Gollin, David Thomas, and Ray Miles for their mentorship, and Professor Michael Wertheimer for the same and for many, many hours of conversation and collaboration on Gestalt psychology and on related issues critical to this work. I would also like to thank Professors R. Allen Gardner, F.I.M. Craik, and R. Reed Hunt for their excellent critical thoughts on many of the issues considered in this work, and my father, Joseph A. Sharps, United States Geological Survey retired, for numerous conversations and thoughts about the adaptive significance of things cognitive. I would like to extend my thanks to Dr. Jared Jobe and the National Institute on Aging for their support, both intellectual and financial, of the research discussed in chapters 1 and 2. Thanks also to Dr. Aroldo Rodrigues, and a very special thanks to Dean K.P. Wong of the College of Science and Mathematics for his steadfast interest, encouragement, and support of this research over the years. I would also like to extend my very sincere gratitude to Dr. Irving Louis Horowitz and to Dr. Nathaniel J. Pallone for their extraordinarily insightful comments, advice, and help in bringing

these ideas to light. I would also like to extend my gratitude to Laurence Mintz at Transaction for his outstanding diligence, expertise, and professionalism in editing this volume. Finally, I would like to thank my daughter, Tina Kipp, and most especially my wife and colleague, Dr. Jana L. Price-Sharps, for everything.

Introduction

There are walls in the mind.

The walls are of different types. They exist and have their effects in different realms.

There is a wall between the memory capabilities of a young person and those of the same person as he or she grows older. The effect of this wall is saddening, as one contemplates the gradual loss of the mental sharpness that characterizes youth.

There are walls between the representations of visual information, auditory information, and verbal information. The effect of these walls is perplexing, as one tries to understand how one can think at all if these different sources of input are divided in the mind.

There are frequently walls between the processes involved in making decisions and the information needed to make good ones. This, oddly enough, may be true even if decision-makers already possess the necessary information in long-term memory. The effect of these walls can be catastrophic.

That such walls exist at all is a puzzle. The mind derives from the brain; it is the functional consequence of the brain's electrochemical activity. The brain is a unitary thing. Granted, there are different anatomical areas of the brain which have different functions, and there are different neurotransmitters which are involved in different activities. Nevertheless, in a constantly active electrochemical organ a few centimeters across, an organ which specializes in a monumental and almost incredible degree of interconnectivity, it is difficult to see how these walls are maintained.

An even more interesting question is how to make them go away.

The idea of "walls" presented here, of course, is merely a metaphor for the types of functional barriers which may result in diminished cognitive processing, or in cognitive processing which is inadequate to meet a given set of task demands. These "walls" are not suggested to be physical, anatomical barriers; a century of solid neurological and neuropsychological research has shown this not to be

1

the case. Rather, such barriers must be functional consequences of something the brain is doing; they must be consequences of the brain's electrochemical activity. But if that electrochemical activity tends to be relatively uniform, at least in terms of the similar functions of neurons and neuronal subsystems, then how can functional barriers between one type of functioning and another, or between cognitive processes and the information which would facilitate those processes, exist at the experiential or psychological level?

These are the subjects of the present volume. The book presents the results of a long-term research program in cognitive aging, mental representation, and cognitive processing. The major finding of this research, deriving from several subfields of cognitive psychology, is that the "walls" in the mind, the functional barriers which must in some way arise as a consequence of neural activity, do not exist at all, at least not as discrete, enduring, reifiable entities. Rather, such barriers exist as epiphenomena of the ways in which brains are required to operate by their owners, as individual human beings encounter different situations that create different types of task demand. Ultimately, it will be argued that these "walls" in the mind may exist largely as a result of a specific aspect of information processing. Whether such barriers are present in a given processing situation depends upon the degree to which a given representation or decision space is processed with reference to its intrinsic features, and with reference to those features which connect it to both internal and external contexts, as opposed to being processed in a more holistic or "Gestalt" manner, as defined and described below. The evidence for this perspective is presented in the pages that follow. The reader must decide the degree to which this case has been successfully made.

Chapter 1 of this volume presents the basic issues, and the primary axioms and hypotheses on which this work is based. Chapters 2 and 3 present evidence of the effects of cognitive task demand characteristics on the malleability and mutability of visual and verbal representations across the adult life span. Chapter 2 deals with spatial cognition, and chapter 3 with the nonspatial realm. A detailed examination of the evidence presented in these chapters is likely to be of greatest interest to students and professional scholars in the field of cognitive aging, but the most important message of these chapters is that the "walls," the functional barriers, inherent in the aging process can be predictably and systematically strength-

ened, weakened, or eliminated, through the imposition of specific task demand manipulations along specific continua of information characteristics.

Chapter 4 carries these arguments further, demonstrating a functional continuum linking the visual and verbal representational realms. This is accomplished through the use of an intermediate type of representation, nonverbal nonmusical auditory imagery, as a model system. Chapter 5 demonstrates that this continuum exists across stimulus types predominantly as a function of the degree to which feature-intensive or more "Gestalt" processing is emphasized by a given set of task demands or experimental framework. The use of the term "Gestalt" to describe this type of processing, and the relationship of this use of the term and of the theory involved to classical Gestalt concepts, is discussed in Chapter 5 and further considered in chapter 6. Finally, in chapter 6, these considerations are applied to the realm of real-world decision making. Research presented in chapter 6 shows that human understanding of the negative consequences of bad decisions may be significantly and systematically improved by the breaking down of yet another "wall." This wall, this functional barrier, exists between a given decision space and the decider's own knowledge, knowledge that can significantly improve decision understanding if the wall is broken down. In other words, decision making can be significantly enhanced if the functional barrier between the task demands of the given processing event, and the information needed for the success of that event, can be attenuated. It is shown that this may be accomplished by means of simple experimental manipulations which make necessary information immediately available in decision contexts.

It is not suggested that the material presented in this slim volume provides the final answers to the resounding questions of representation and processing. Indeed, it is probable that many of the suggestions advanced below will require modification or rejection as research in the field continues. However, the research presented is the product of seventeen years' systematic empirical evaluation of these issues, and the theoretical considerations advanced are consistent with the results of this research program and with the vast majority of related findings in the field. At the least, this volume is intended to encourage additional research in the relevant venues, research that will contribute more to our understanding of the crucial areas of representation, processing, and decision making.

1

The Paradox of Human Intelligence

In the summer of 2001, extraordinarily high numbers of shark attacks, some of them fatal, were recorded on the southeastern coasts of the United States. These were well publicized. Despite this, people continued to swim in the sea off the shark-infested beaches. In at least one case, a teenager saw the shark which attacked him before it became aggressive, but even in view of the recent attacks, he thought, "Just a shark; probably won't bug me" (Bee Nation Briefs, 2001).

During that same summer, a number of people in Australia, encountering a dead whale being eaten by sharks, actually walked on the whale's body while it was being consumed and petted its voracious consumers. Some of these people brought their children (Associated Press, 2001). At least one person was carrying a baby while petting the feeding sharks in question.

Also recently (Cowen, 1999), a sophisticated space mission was undertaken by NASA for the purpose of sending a spacecraft to Mars. This spacecraft was intended to orbit around the planet, photograph it, and transmit the information gained to the operators on Earth. Even a rough acquaintance with college physics allows one to understand the complexity of such an operation: enabling a rocket to escape Earth's gravity while still maintaining pressures low enough for the survival of the equipment; injecting the vehicle into a pathway which takes into account the gravity of the sun as well as that of both Earth and Mars; slowing the vehicle to the degree needed for proper injection into a useful orbit around Mars, and obtaining the necessary attitude for observation. All of these activities obviously require high intelligence on the part of the operators and mission planners, to say nothing of the abilities required to create the spacecraft and the rocket to deliver it in the first place. Yet the spacecraft was lost as it was maneuvered in space. The reason was a simple failure on the part of the vehicle's controllers to convert from En-

glish units of measurement to the metric units required by the orbiter's programming. This resulted in catastrophic shifts in the vehicle's velocity and orientation, and in the subsequent loss of the spacecraft.

In effect, the NASA operators, literally rocket scientists, "forgot to carry the two."

How can people see sharks in dangerous waters and fail to act accordingly? How can highly intelligent experts make a simple mathematical error that results in the loss of a spacecraft?

In a related question, how can eyewitnesses to crimes make the fantastic numbers of errors of recall that have been documented, resulting in wrongful convictions (e.g., Sporer, Malpass & Koehnken, 1996)? Very frequently, the representations of criminals and crime scenes carried in the memories of witnesses are shockingly flawed. Psychologists serving as expert witnesses in the courtroom, including the present author, have repeatedly seen suspects originally described as blond and light-complexioned turn out to be dark brunettes, and vice versa. Semi-automatic pistols have turned into revolvers in the elastic memories of witnesses, then literally into ice picks, then back into handguns of indiscriminate features. Black trousers and white t-shirts have become light blue jeans and striped Oxford button-downs. Et cetera.

Some, but not all, of these types of errors may be exacerbated with age. Older adults do not, as a rule and on average, remember as well as young people do. Yet this statement must be qualified; older adults, for example, tend to possess verbal abilities under many task conditions which are preserved relative to their abilities to process images and pictures (Dror & Kosslyn, 1994; Nebes, 1990; Sharps, 1990; but see also Hertzog et al., 1993). This is not, of course, to say that older adults do not exhibit verbal memory deficits relative to young people; they certainly do, especially when provided with more syntactically complex verbal stimulus materials (e.g., Craik & Jennings, 1992; Hertzog et al., 1993; Light, 1990). However, it can be said that under a number of experimental circumstances, most notably the Brown-Peterson task (Brown, 1958; Craik, 1977; Peterson & Peterson, 1959) and even in some types of memory for text (see Ahlberg & Sharps, in press), the admittedly extant memory deficits that occur with age are not typically found to be as large or profound as those found in the pictorial realm, especially when complex pictures are utilized (e.g., Dror & Kosslyn, 1994; Sharps &

Gollin, 1987a,b; Sharps, 1990, 1991, 1997, 1998). Even in the face of relatively poor pictorial memory, however, the recall performance of older adults in the pictorial realm can be artificially enhanced to the level enjoyed by the young (e.g., Waddell & Rogoff, 1981; McCormack, 1982; Sharps & Gollin, 1987a, 1988) if older adults are presented with appropriate stimulus conditions.

Consider also the fact that although some aspects of the memory of older adults may be deficient when compared to the memory powers of young adults, the reasoning powers of the aged, which ultimately must depend on their memories and metamemories, can in many contexts equal or exceed those of the young. This is especially true in those realms typically subsumed under the popular sobriquet of "wisdom" (Simonton, 1990), although, of course, there are contexts (such as spatial reasoning) in which age-related disparities exist (e.g., Salthouse, 1992).

How can these paradoxes of cognitive aging exist? If older adult memory deteriorates simply because of some sort of wear-and-tear inherent in the aging process, than why do some kinds of memory deteriorate more than others? And how can some types of reasoning fail to deteriorate at all? Reasoning by definition involves the processing of information. If the ability to remember that information is damaged, then how can reasoning performance itself exhibit no sign of this damage? There are mysteries here which wholly eclipse the concept that the mind "naturally" deteriorates with age.

Although failures to reason properly about sharks and spacecraft may initially seem unrelated to failures to remember suspects properly, and these in turn may appear unrelated to the difficulties with memory experienced by older adults, they are, in fact, very much interconnected. As will be discussed in this volume, the common denominator lies in the area of *representation*. There are fundamental commonalities in memory and thinking which must be understood if either type of cognitive activity is to be fully comprehended, and which are perhaps best understood, at least at a preliminary level, through an examination of cognitive aging as a model system.

Obviously, some of the cases cited above might be idiosyncratic. The teenager with the shark might have had something else on his mind. The people walking on the dead whale might have been inundated with the recent glut of televised nature programs extolling the harmlessness of giant carnivorous sharks. The NASA scientists and engineers might have had too many technical issues dividing their

attention, or they might have been focused on agency politics at the time. There are obviously many competing possibilities in any given case of intellectual error. Yet the types of errors cited above, in which intelligent or at least reasonably intelligent people commit significant errors of judgement or memory, are sufficiently common to warrant psychological attention. It is also true that the perplexing and paradoxical age-related effects described above have been repeatedly and empirically confirmed.

Can these types of errors be explained in simple terms of failures to "pay attention?" A number of elegant attentional explanations for "absent-mindedness" (Baddeley, 2001) of a type that might be relevant here have been suggested over the years (e.g., Norman and Shallice, 1986; Reason, 1984; Shallice, 1982). Yet attentional anomalies cannot explain the radical reconfiguration of memory representations often seen in eyewitness identification errors, and it is difficult to see how one *could* fail to pay attention to the negative prospects of close contact with sharks, especially when the sharks in question are currently eating the whale one is standing on.

This is not to say that attentional processes are not involved in these types of events. They certainly are. But even so, we are still faced with the same fundamental question. If information is already present in the mind at some level, how can we fail to access that information as the need arises?

Cognitive errors, failures of memory and reasoning, occur across the life span. At least within some cognitive realms, their frequencies and magnitudes typically increase with age. But even in the young or the relatively young, such errors are by no means confined to situations in which quick thinking might be needed, as in a shark attack, or in very complex situations requiring enormous division of attention, as in a NASA control room, or even in situations in which strong emotions might play a part, as in a criminal courtroom. Such errors are observed even under conditions in which intelligent people have plenty of time to make their judgments.

In some cases, these errors are literally set in stone, or at least in brick. One of the lesser-known tourist attractions of San Francisco lies directly beneath the Golden Gate Bridge, on the southern shore of San Francisco Bay from which the Golden Gate issues north to Marin. It is Fort Point, a nineteenth-century artillery post that used to guard the bay against the possibility of invasion from the sea. The visitor can see the enormous walls and the intricate coast artillery

guns themselves, still seated on their carriages in different places around the fort. One cannot fail to be impressed by the ingenuity, the *intelligence*, that must have been involved in the construction of the great coastal defense guns (see Burgin, 2000; Manucy, 1949/ 1985; National Park Service, 2000). The perfect shaping of the barrels to withstand the enormous pressures which developed in their rifled interiors; the clever sliding mechanisms which allowed the gigantic weapons to recoil without destroying their carriages; the intricate gearing and wheel mechanisms which allowed their crews to turn the great steel carriages themselves, using muscle power alone; all of these reflect the near-apotheosis of nineteenth-century ingenuity. These guns are cleverly designed, nearly perfect for their purpose, "pushing the envelope" of the materials available to nineteenth-century engineers. It is obvious, to any thinking observer, that these mighty weapons were designed by *really smart people*.

Who then put them inside a brick fort?

Yes, brick. Fort Point, like a number of other forts constructed around the same time, was made out of bricks, which rifled artillery on ships or elsewhere would have crumbled into dust with a few well-placed salvos. A prolonged series of salvos could have pulverized the entire fort. An interesting paradox emerges: the brilliant engineering of the guns was accompanied by the almost incredibly foolish placement of the same guns in a completely worthless defensive facility. The fort was effectively obsolete, literally before it was build.

A considerable period of time and a considerable amount of thought went into both the guns and the fort; here we do not see the rush of a shark attack, or the extraordinary complexity of a NASA mission. Yet the end result proved very similar. The finest weapons of the day were placed inside a facility which would admittedly have given medieval knights a run for their money, but which would have been destroyed very swiftly if faced by any weapons similar to those which the fort itself was built to house.

One can also see the great main door of the fort, intricately set with metal studs of the type used in the medieval world to fend off battle-axes. Fort Point is effectively a fortress of the Middle Ages, dropped into the middle of the nineteenth century and expected to defend itself; and as a thoughtful observer contemplates this literally concrete example of the paradox of human intelligence, especially in its setting beneath the brilliantly intricate buttressing of the Golden

Gate itself, one must ask the question:

"What could they possibly have been thinking?"

This question summarizes the most important puzzle confronting modern cognitive psychology, the central paradox of human intelligence: How can people do brilliant things, but at the same time do stupid ones? How can people create brilliant weapons and then place them inside a useless fort? For that matter, how can people create a clever pesticide and then spread it around the environment to the point that its creators have to breathe it too? How can people develop the medical and agricultural technology that makes it possible to overpopulate a world, and then be dumb enough, so to speak, to actually *do* it? In a world of six billion human souls and rising, these questions lie not only at the heart of cognitive psychology, but also at the heart of human survival and quality of life on this planet.

This volume represents an attempt to address these questions. It does not provide a complete answer, nor necessarily the only answer. It is very probable that many of the details will prove to require modification, or will simply prove to be wrong. However, the data presented here, gleaned over seventeen years of experimental research, are at least internally consistent and consistent with the state of current knowledge. It is hoped that this volume will, at the least, encourage more research into these fundamental questions of the intellect.

On the Nature of Mind

Any consideration of this type is immediately faced with the problem of the basic architecture of cognition. How are cognitive processes arranged so that errors of the types described are even possible? Both logic and a consideration of the available literature must be used to form even a partial conception of this issue.

First, some logical consideration is needed. It is doubtful, indeed impossible, that any adult in the modern world is unaware that sharks can be dangerous. It is also doubtful that anyone is unaware that sharks eat meat, that whales are largely made of meat, that people are also made largely of meat, and that therefore standing on top of a whale currently undergoing consumption by sharks is a genuinely bad idea. It is also somewhat incredible that NASA scientists would have been unaware of the units of measurement used in programming their equipment.

These considerations lead to what might be called the first axiom of the present work: *Information can be available in memory and yet have no effect on a given decision. Even if information is known, it may not influence a decision for which it would be relevant.* Bad decisions are not only made in ignorance. Sometimes they are made even when information that should have prevented those decisions is known to the subject.

Now, in the absence of other determining factors (vested interest, emotional investment, etc.), this must mean that although relevant information is present in memory, it is not present in the immediate computational environment of the decision in question. This implies the existence of separable processing systems, in which these cognitive processes can proceed in isolation from one another; in effect, there is a strong suggestion of some sort of multistore processing system. The bad decision or thinking process is going on in one metaphorical cognitive space, and the necessary information which would prevent the bad decision or outcome is irrelevant because it is resident, somehow, in another. This concept would also help to explain the many of the mysteries still present in the cognitive aging literature; if one type of storage system were more susceptible to the negative effects of aging than another, then the different effects of the aging process which have been empirically observed with regard to different cognitive subsystems would of course be logically defensible.

Multistore models are hardly unfamiliar in cognitive psychology. The most redoubtable is probably that of Atkinson and Schiffrin (1968), which in one way or another still pervades the field, although the older concept of short-term memory (STM) has largely given way to the multistore-system of working memory (e.g., Baddeley, 1986). A variety of new strictures, restraints, emendations and modifications have been added to this model, especially given much evidence in the levels-of-processing tradition (e.g., Craik and Lockhart, 1972) that the boundaries between short- and long-term memory (LTM), and the connections between the two, are by no means as adamantine as originally conceived. However, there is no serious question that immediate memory has different characteristics than does memory over hours or weeks, or that either STM or LTM differ from the sensory store of the first half-second after stimulation. There are reasonable, empirically based distinctions among information systems in the human mind. The types of cognitive architecture which

would be required to support the first axiom given above therefore can, and do, exist: there are divisions in the mind, as exemplified by the contrasting characteristics of relatively immediate and relatively long-term memory.

A more important division for present purposes, and the one used as a model system in the majority of the work to be discussed, lies between verbal and pictorial processing. An enormous body of research in the tradition of Paivio (e.g., 1971, 1975, 1990) has shown that verbal and imageric information are processed in fundamentally different ways (e.g., Kosslyn, 1980; Paivio, 1990; Shepard & Metzler, 1971).

So, given the existence of evidence of different subsystems based on the amount of time elapsed after encoding (sensory, working, and long-term memory), and the evident existence of processing distinctions based on the type of stimuli initially encoded (for example, verbal or pictorial materials), it seems unlikely that there will be much objection to the second axiom driving the present work: *There must be divisions, inherent in information processing, between the processing of different kinds of information (e.g., pictorial and verbal), divisions which allow different kinds of information to be processed and to exist in relative isolation from one another.*

But this comfortable and well-supported axiom in fact leads to a major difficulty. Although most modern authorities are in agreement, for example, that imagery and verbal processing are carried on in functionally interdependent but nevertheless separable systems (e.g., Paivio, 1990), one searches current literature on the neurological substrate of cognition in vain for a possible mechanism of such separation. It is of course true that images and words are primarily processed in different gross anatomical regions of the brain. However, and this might be taken as the third axiom, *the ultimate nature of the representation of both kinds of information, indeed of all kinds of information, must lie in the electrochemical activity of the brain's neurons.*

So, there is a difficulty. Images and words are experienced differently by the given subject, and they are apparently processed differently. Yet ultimately they must be the same *kind* of information across anatomical regions of the brain itself, resident in the electrochemical activity of the brain's neurons.

This dilemma could perhaps be resolved in part by means of an analogy from the purely biological realm: the ultimate-versus-proxi-

mate cause model of Mayr (e.g., 1982). The basic concept is that there are both ultimate and proximate causes of any given biological phenomenon. If one is drinking water, the proximate cause is a feeling of thirst. Ultimate causes include the facts that one is a mammal for whom regular water is required, the fact that one's genes have ultimately coded for all of the proteins in the muscles used to drink, the fact that water exists at all, and so on. Obviously this is not a concrete dichotomy, but a continuum. For example, the activation of the thirst receptors, the hypothalamic involvement in thirst production, and the internal monitoring of blood volume are all factors which partake both of ultimate and proximate causality in the case of the thirst example. There are many factors whose influence lies somewhere between the ultimate and proximate levels.

How can such a relatively amorphous concept be of help, even analogously, in untangling the current dilemma? What is proposed here, as a "fourth axiom" which is not in fact an axiom at all but a thesis deriving from the first three, is that *information must have both an ultimate and a proximate nature*, which admittedly, of course, would be expected to grade into one another. The ultimate end of this continuum would lie in the basic electrophysiological activity of the brain. The proximate end would lie in the type of information (verbal, imageric, and so on) that is being processed, and, even more "proximately," in the subject's verifiable experience of that information, in the psychological and experiential realms. Again, of course, some level of continuity between the ultimate and proximate nature of information would naturally be expected.

If these considerations are accurate, then something about the nature of cognitive processing itself, rather than of the basic electrophysiological impulses that constitute the ultimate level, must result in the differences among information types that manifest themselves at the proximate level. This suggests the hypothesis (not an axiom or thesis) driving the work to be discussed below. This hypothesis is that *it is the demand characteristics of the given cognitive task that determine the proximate, or experiential, nature of the information in question*. This is postulated to be the source of the common factors among the situations discussed above, the isolation of different kinds of information from one another in the processes of thinking and memory.

In other words, items as encoded are experienced, for example, as primarily pictorial or primarily verbal. However, at the ultimate

level of storage in the brain, the relatively unitary character of representation, necessitated by the relatively unitary character of the electrochemical mechanisms of representation, "blends" the stimulus characteristics. It is this blend, rather than a veridical copy of the initial stimulus input, that returns at retrieval. Thus a given pictorial item, for example, might be modified by a respondent's memory of a verbal description of that item, or of verbal descriptions of similar items, or even of the category to which that item belongs.

This idea, if demonstrated to be correct, would have the power to explain a variety of the current mysteries of cognitive psychology and of cognitive aging. The difference between memory for verbal and for pictorial material, for example, might not lie predominantly in differences in the anatomical substrates; it might instead lie in the nature of the cognitive activity involved. Failures of reasoning, such as the shark, spacecraft, and fort examples cited above, would be cases in which the given subject simply failed to do something specific to the available information, something that would result in its access-and-processing rather than merely in its maintenance. In effect, these failures may represent the instantiation of processing "programs" for the wrong kinds of demand characteristics. Older adults might differ from the young in their ability to engage in specific types of cognitive activity which are needed, not for memory or reasoning per se, but to deal with the demand characteristics of specific, but different, processing tasks.

Similar hypothetical processes would also explain much of the difficulty observed in eyewitness identification. Cognitive task demand characteristics may be as crucial as, or more crucial than, basic representational factors in memory. If so, then one's memory of, for example, an automatic pistol might ultimately be rendered as an abstract concept such as "gun" or even "weapon," a concept *which could take on different levels or types of imageric or verbal properties at the proximate level, depending upon the demand characteristics of the given retrieval task.* Substitutions of revolvers and even ice picks for automatics at retrieval would then be explicable. If task-specific demand characteristics, which require the accessing of a given piece of information, are as important as, or more important than, the original nature of the information encoded at the experiential level, then the way in which that information is accessed and reported may be quite variable, as is demonstrated on a daily basis in criminal courtrooms. Pictorial information and verbal informa-

tion may actually be interchangeable, to some degree and at some level, and may metamorphose into one another under specific cognitive circumstances and under the task demands of specific retrieval and processing situations.

Obviously these are hypotheses which require empirical evidence. This is the primary purpose of the present volume: to present the evidence that supports these concepts. This evidence derives from the work of others and from that of the author, colleagues and students over seventeen years in three specific areas: the study of cognitive aging, the study of auditory and visual imagery in memory, and the study of visual-spatial processing within the venerable mental rotation paradigm. The relevant findings are presented below.

2

Minds through Time I: What Aging and Spatial Cognition Reveal about the Nature of Representation

The aging process provides valuable insights into the phenomena of memory and reasoning. Aging results in a linear and irreversible motion of the mind through time. The changes in mind that occur during this temporal journey tell us about the nature of representation and thought, and about the ways in which information processing systems are segregated one from the other, or are integrated together, depending upon the cognitive tasks for which they are used.

Why, specifically, is the aging process useful in this regard? First, it should be stated that the study of cognitive aging is of great importance in its own right, of course, simply because of the practical importance of the work. All human beings age, and great numbers of people fear the inevitable changes brought about by the aging process. A clear and accurate understanding of aging, including cognitive aging, is therefore of obvious importance, simply as a contribution to the quality of human life across the life span.

However, it is a more academic attribute of the study of cognitive aging that concerns us here. Older adults, as a result of specific cognitive changes, constitute virtually ideal "preparations" for the study of specific cognitive processes, for the examination of a kind of natural "reverse engineering" of cognition itself as the brain changes with age. Several of the important divisions between different types of human information processing are magnified by the aging process, which therefore provides a dynamic model system for the examination of these divisions as they change with age.

As discussed briefly above, one of those age differences, of particular salience here, is an average age difference in the processing of verbal materials and of visual-spatial, pictorial stimulus materials.

Age-related changes in the relationship between the representation of these two types of stimuli provide a literally ideal testing ground for several of the concepts discussed to this point.

Older adults, on average, retain relatively better verbal processing than they do visual-spatial abilities, although there are differences in the degree of change in the visual-spatial realm, depending upon the tests or task demands to which the research participants are subjected (e.g., Hertzog et al., 1993; Salthouse, 1995; Smith & Park, 1990). An understanding of the processing décalage between the verbal and visual-spatial realms would clearly contribute profoundly to the question of representation, which in turn would make it possible to understand how important information can be isolated from the immediate cognitive environment of a decision-making process. The nature of imageric and verbal processing in older adults provides a simpler, more accessible model system for the more complex realm of information isolation in decision making, and therefore forms the starting point for the present research. But in order to make the necessary examination of this distinction within cognitive aging, it is first necessary to understand why the memory processing of older adults changes in the ways that it does.

Cognitive Processing in the Normal Aging Mind

Although it is generally acknowledged that normal aging diminishes the average person's powers of memory, it has proven surprisingly difficult to determine why this is the case. As discussed above, changes in memory are not uniform. Older adults perform more poorly than do young adults on some tasks, but may achieve parity on others (e.g., Craik, 1986; Park, Cherry, Smith & Lafronza, 1990; Sharps, 1991; Waddell & Rogoff, 1981). What are the common denominators underlying these apparently contradictory findings?

Research since 1984 by the author, colleagues, and students has resulted in a synthetic theory of cognitive aging, the *Cognitive Asynchrony Theory* (Sharps, 1998), that makes it possible to reconcile the various findings reported in the literature, and at the same time to shed light on the fundamental question of representation. This theory requires an understanding of three current theoretical perspectives in aging and cognition:

1.   The generalized slowing hypothesis (e.g., Birren, 1974; Cerella, 1985; Salthouse, 1982, 1985, 1994a, b), which holds that older adults are

subject to a gradual diminution of the speed with which information can be processed.

2. Environmental support theory (e.g., Craik, 1986, 1994; Craik & Jennings, 1992), which holds that, due to age-related reduction of the ability to utilize self-initiated processing, older adults may benefit more than young adults from external support for memory.

3. Item-specific/relational information theory (Einstein & Hunt, 1980; Hunt & Einstein, 1981), which holds that there are functional processing distinctions between information specific to individual stimulus items (item-specific information, such as certain visual details) and information which is shared between items (relational information, such as category membership).

The first of these perspectives, generalized slowing (e.g., Birren, Riegel, & Morrison, 1962; Birren, 1974), holds that as an individual ages, the speed with which neural impulses can be delivered to their destinations within the brain diminishes. This process results from essentially random forces. Cerella (1990) holds that the generalized slowing observed as a function of age results from the random breaking of neural "links," resulting in diminished reaction times according to the formula

$$L = \mu\ N,$$

where L is reaction time (latency), μ is the time required by each step of a given process, and N is the number of links involved in the process. The resultant generalized slowing probably exerts much of its effect through working memory (Salthouse, 1994a).

Cognitive asynchrony theory (Sharps, 1998; Sharps, Foster, Martin, & Nunes, 1999; Sharps, Martin, Nunes, & Merrill, 1999) holds that given the random nature of the processes involved, the loss of neural linkages cannot be uniform. This loss results from effectively chaotic forces inherent in the normal aging process. This means that some subsystems will diminish more than others simply as the result of random chance, with the end result that there will be a gradual and increasing asynchrony among subsystems. In a simplified example, information in a young brain might arrive at a given brain destination all at once when ten hypothetical subsystems work in unison. However, in an aging brain with greater loss in some subsystems than in others, that information would arrive in three or four segments: five of the ten systems might operate in unison as before,

but several others would be slowed to different rates by different levels of cell loss, and one or two would operate even more slowly.

This asynchrony means that those memories which require more simultaneous inputs for encoding or retrieval will be more profoundly influenced for the worse in older adults. This is in fact known to be the case (Birren, Riegel & Morrison, 1962:10): age differences in processing speed tend to increase when greater degrees of manipulation or consideration are needed before subjects are able to respond to any given stimulus situation.

Therefore, complex mental images, resulting from complex percepts in the real world, should be more difficult for an older person to process than should simple ones, and simple images in turn should prove more difficult than verbal propositions such as words. Complex images need more synchronized or simultaneous inputs for complete processing than do simple images. Simple images require synchronized or simultaneous inputs more than do words, which are abstractions, embedded in semantic networks but possessing no intrinsic item-specific detail. In other words, an image has more detail, requiring greater synchronization of a greater summative amount of input, than does a corresponding word. Therefore, the details of verbal materials should prove to be more readily processed than those of pictorial materials, given that a verbal trace possesses and gives rise to fewer item-specific details (see Hunt & Einstein, 1981) than does a pictorial trace. Pictures possess colors, textures, and specific features that words, no matter how evocative of imagery, cannot.

The processing difference between verbal and pictorial materials was demonstrated by Paivio and colleagues (e.g., Paivio & Csapo, 1969; Paivio, 1975, 1990). An important demonstration of this principle (Paivio, 1975), showed that pictures which were incompatible in terms of relative size (such as a drawing of a very large table lamp next to a very small zebra, so that the lamp was larger than the zebra) required more time to process than did pictures which bore the normal expected relative dimensions. However, *words* which bore an incongruity (the word "lamp" printed in large type next to the word "zebra" in a small type font, for example) produced the same reaction times as did words in normal format. This showed that the details of a verbal item are of less relevance, in processing terms, than the details of a picture; the alteration of a specific detail (relative size) was deleterious to the processing of pictures, but had no effect on the processing of words.

Nervous systems slow with age. This slowing proceeds in an asynchronous manner. Asynchronous slowing will more profoundly diminish the processing of more specifically detailed stimuli (such as pictures) than of less detailed items (such as words). Given these facts, one would expect poorer performance in a gradually slowing, and hence gradually asynchronous, nervous system when it deals with pictorial stimuli than when it deals with verbal information. Older adults, on average, should therefore have more trouble remembering visual-spatial materials, by comparison with verbal information, than do younger people.

They do. Dror and Kosslyn (1994) demonstrated that older adults exhibit significant deficits in pictorial processing relative to young people, and there is also a considerable body of evidence (e.g., Nebes, 1990) that semantic systems, predominantly verbal in nature, are *relatively* well preserved through the normal aging process. Semantic, meaningful encoding processes have not, in many studies, been found to be impaired by advancing age (e.g., Duchek, 1984; McDowd & Craik, 1988; but see also Lorsbach & Simpson, 1988; Salthouse, 1988). Light (1990:281) suggests "no support for the claim that deficits in semantic processing underlie memory problems in old age," although retrieval of particular words and the planning of verbal statements may diminish with age (Mackay & Abrams, 1996). So, it does in fact appear that the more detail-intensive pictorial realm is typically more susceptible to the negative influences of the aging process than is less detail-intensive verbal processing, although, as mentioned above, there is some degree of age-related loss in both areas.

If generalized cognitive slowing, and subsequent cognitive asynchrony, are the sources of these age-related discrepancies in the processing of verbal and pictorial materials, then it should be possible, experimentally, to alter levels of performance in these areas in young and older adults. Consideration of Craik's environmental support theory (e.g., 1986, 1994) suggests ways of doing this. For Craik, older persons are likely to be deficient in self-initiated processing. In memory tasks which provide relatively little environmental support, individual subjects have to rely more heavily on their own self-initiated operations if they are to retrieve information successfully. Craik argues that these self-initiated operations become increasingly difficult with advancing age. This is the reason that some experimental tasks produce large age differences in memory, and others

produce small differences or none at all; the crucial factor is the degree of self-initiated processing required by the given task (Craik, 1986:419).

Older adults should therefore experience more difficulty with cognitive tasks that require significant reliance on internal resources. On the other hand, tasks that depend more upon external or environmental support should be easier for older adults to deal with. An example of this lies in the difference between recognition, cued recall, and free recall (e.g., Craik, 1986; Craik & McDowd, 1987). In recognition, one simply has to recognize what has been seen before. The details that were present at encoding are physically present in the subject's environment at retrieval, and therefore little self-initiated activity is required. Recognition memory tasks provide a high level of external support. In free recall, on the other hand, *none* of the details of encoding are physically present at retrieval. To retrieve, one must generate the memory internally. Free recall is a task that provides little or no environmental support. Cued recall, which presents a *portion* of the details of a given encoding situation in the external environment at retrieval, would fall somewhere between these extremes. Given this continuum of self-initiated processing from recognition to free recall, age-related memory performance gaps should be large in free recall, small in recognition, and intermediate in cued recall; this is in fact the case (e.g., Craik, 1986; Craik & McDowd, 1987). Older adults can make use of external support, such as that provided by recognition memory tasks, to improve their recall.

So, it should be possible to compensate for the deficits observed in visuospatial memory by means of environmental support. In other words, one might compensate for older adults' difficulty in processing the details of visual-spatial stimuli by rendering those details more distinctive at encoding. This hypothesis is especially important in light of the idea that a major component of age-related loss in visual memory derives from asynchronous speed loss. If cognitive speed and synchrony are needed to maintain the intact pictorial memory abilities of young adults, then as speed and neural synchrony are lost with aging, it should be possible to compensate for these losses. This could be done through the use of increased levels of environmental support, since enhanced distinctiveness would be assumed to recruit more neural resources, which in turn would result in diminished effects of asynchrony. Evidence in several areas

of visual cognition, presented below, has been provided that this is in fact the case.

Evidence from Mental Rotation

Mental rotation (MR) is not a type of memory, but it involves functions and processes that are critical for visual-spatial memory processing. MR may therefore be used as a model system for those processes. The mental rotation paradigm has proven to be especially useful for examining visuospatial representation and manipulation under speeded and non-speeded conditions.

The elderly generally exhibit poorer MR accuracy than do young adults, and they are slower than their younger counterparts (e.g., Cerella, Poon & Fozard, 1981; Berg, Hertzog, & Hunt, 1982; Hertzog, Vernon & Rypma, 1993). But are older adults really *worse* at processing images, or are they just *slower*? The considerations advanced above suggest two specific hypotheses:

1. The asynchronous speed loss typical of normal aging is a primary cause of the MR decline. Therefore, if speed demands are absent, MR performance in older adults should improve.

2. The asynchrony of generalized slowing is suggested to render complex images relatively difficult to process for older adults. Therefore, complex MR images should require more time to process than simple ones, and this should be more pronounced in older than in younger adults.

Two experiments tested these hypotheses. In the first (Sharps & Gollin, 1987a), twenty-seven young adults and twenty-seven older people (mean age nineteen and seventy-one years, respectively), were presented with twenty-two standard abstract Shepard-Metzler MR items (Shepard & Metzler, 1971). As is well known, the goal of the MR task is to rotate two elements of a given item into congruence in order to tell whether the two elements are identical or stereoisomers.

Participants were divided into three groups. One group of young and one group of older adults received instructions, typical of those used in MR studies, to rotate the items "as quickly as possible." A second group at each age level, however, received no instructions concerning speed, being told merely to do the task "as accurately as possible." A third group was required to "balance" speed and accuracy in their rotations.

The results were entirely consistent with the hypothesis that it was speed loss, rather than some unspecified "imagery" component of the MR task, that rendered older adults less able. Not surprisingly, in the "speed" condition, older adults, achieving the same speeds of rotation as young adults, performed more poorly in their judgments of identity versus stereoisomeric difference. However, in the "accuracy" condition, older adults *were as accurate as young adults* in making their judgments, although they took far longer to make them. In the speed/accuracy "balance" condition, interestingly, older adults were still as accurate as the young. However, elders took significantly longer than young adults to make these judgements. Also, elders in the "balance" condition did not take as long as did the elders in the pure "accuracy" condition.

In sum, these results showed that older adults' mental rotation performance can be as good as that of college-aged individuals, provided that speed requirements are deleted or minimized. It is speed requirements, not loss of "imagery abilities," that results in age-related difficulties with this task. This was precisely the result predicted by Hypothesis 1 above, that the asynchronous speed loss typical of normal aging is a source of MR decline, and that the absence of speed demands would reduce age-related loss in the accuracy of MR performance.

It must be noted that these results are task dependent (e.g., Gaylord & Marsh, 1975; Herman & Bruce, 1983; Wilson et al. 1975). These issues are treated in depth in earlier papers (Sharps, 1990; Sharps, 1998). The Sharps and Gollin (1987a) results reported here, however, serve to underscore the critical point for present purposes: in a "bare-bones" MR task, without contributing fatigue or format factors, older adults were capable of generating the same accuracy as the young, provided that speed was not an issue, exactly as predicted.

What about the second hypothesis, that age-related speed loss would result in cognitive asynchrony and therefore in relative difficulty for elders in more complex processing? There is evidence for this "complexity hypothesis." Cerella, Poon, and Williams (1980), in a review of the literature, found that increasingly complex tasks tend to increase reaction times for elders. Indeed, for adults of all ages, more complex MR tasks generally require more time to complete (e.g., Bethell-Fox & Shepard, 1988; Cooper, 1975; Cooper & Podgorny, 1976; Folk & Luce, 1987; Herman & Bruce, 1983; Shepard

& Metzler, 1988; Yuille & Steiger, 1982), especially with three-dimensional figures (e.g., Jolicoeur et al., 1985; see also Puglisi & Morell, 1986).

The interaction of figural complexity, speed, and age was systematically tested in a study (Sharps, 1990) using modified two-dimensional Shepard-Metzler items which varied in complexity. Recall the prediction that more complex MR figures would result in relatively diminished speed of performance for the elderly, in that the greater visual-spatial demands created by more complex figures would prove especially deleterious for older people. The study exposed twenty-eight young and twenty-eight older adults to these items. Subjects were asked to judge whether the two elements of each figure were the same or different. Speed-accuracy "balance" instructions were given.

As in Sharps and Gollin (1987a), no significant differences in accuracy between young and older adults were observed. However, older adults were significantly slower than the young, and in a manner entirely consistent with the hypotheses advanced: the interactive effect of figural complexity and age was significant on reaction time. The "speed gap" between young and older adults widened significantly as a function of the complexity of the stimulus items, precisely as predicted by the second hypothesis advanced above.

So, the results of these MR manipulations with reference to older adults were consistent with the ideas presented thus far. As proposed, the relative visual-spatial deficit observed in normal aging is intricately tied to age-related generalized slowing, which is especially prevalent in more complex stimulus situations. If more time is provided, or simpler stimulus items are used, age differences in this type of processing diminish or disappear. Consistent with the more general ideas advanced above, there does not appear to be anything particularly "special" about imageric stimuli (at least within the MR framework), as opposed to verbal stimuli, that diminishes older adult performance. Rather, it is the more general processing consideration of speed-related asynchrony *acting* on representations of different stimulus types, not the representations themselves, which produces the observed effects.

The difference between old and young adults in verbal processing has generally been found to be relatively small. The difference in pictorial processing is relatively large. However, consistent with the ideas advanced above, the pictorial difference can be reduced,

made more like the verbal difference, in effect, through simple manipulations of task demand characteristics. While this is hardly definitive proof, it is certainly a strong indication that demand characteristics play a formidable role in the production of experiential differences.

Thus far we have seen these effects only in the circumscribed area of MR. Do these types of effects generalize across tasks? Can similar results be generated in other areas?

Evidence from Spatial Memory

Spatial memory, memory for routes and locations, would have been of great importance in the hunter-gatherer past in which the human species evolved. Virtually all subsistence activities in the pre-agrarian world (tracking, trailing, spearing or shooting, recalling the locations where plant foods grew) were spatial in nature. These abilities must therefore have been of considerable adaptive significance for both individuals and groups.

Given the importance of visual-spatial abilities in the ancient world, and in the absence of paleolithic pensions, retirement plans, and social security, how could ancient peoples have afforded to maintain reasonable populations of older adults who no longer possessed good spatial memory? How could they have supported large numbers of people who were entirely dependent on others for basic food gathering? It seems that in the pre-retirement world, older adults must have maintained a relatively high level of spatial cognitive abilities. Even if older adults were no longer involved in major hunting or gathering behavior, the mending of nets, the production of stone tools and basketry, and the countless other activities of ancient life which absolutely required strong visual-spatial abilities would seem to have precluded major eugeric changes in this realm.

And yet a number of studies, using simple paper maps (e.g., Light & Zelinski, 1983), two-dimensional arrays (e.g., Pezdek, 1983), and other such stimuli have shown that the spatial memory performance of older adults is decidedly worse than that of the young. This seems ecologically very unlikely, given evolutionary demands, and the paradox becomes even more intriguing when other work (e.g., Waddell & Rogoff, 1981), providing contrary results, demonstrating parity of performance between young and older adults, is considered. What is happening here?

Craik's environmental support theory (e.g., Craik, 1986; Craik & Jennings, 1992; Craik & McDowd, 1987) provides a relatively complete and parsimonious answer. A typical procedure in spatial memory tasks is to show young and older adults an array, such as a map of a given space of some kind, with items placed or depicted on the array. The array is then removed, and respondents are provided with another array of the same layout but with the items removed. The respondents are supposed to indicate the remembered locations of the items on the blank arrays.

In such tasks, highly effortful self-initiated processes would probably be critical. Light and Zelinski's (1983) map, for example, was a sparse, black-and-white depiction of a realistic space with landmarks drawn on it. Pezdek's (1983) array was a series of black-and-white drawings of spaces divided into quadrants, and the goal was to recall the correct quadrant of a given item's placement. Such spaces provide few cues to location, and few cues that possess any strong degree of visual distinctiveness for respondents to use to cue locations in memory; thus subjects, including older adults, are forced to rely on their internal images of relatively cue-sparse arrays. This type of task, not surprisingly, routinely results in poor spatial memory performance in older adults.

However, Waddell and Rogoff (1981) found that these results were by no means absolute. Poor spatial memory was not shown to be a characteristic of old age, but of the placement of older adults under *task demands which were suboptimal for their performance*. One of Waddell and Rogoff's (1981) conditions, like those of Pezdek and of Light and Zelinski, resulted in a significant disparity between the performance of middle-aged and older adults. In this condition, respondents were to remember the locations of small objects in a relatively featureless array of boxes. However, when the same objects were arranged in a realistic, small-scale panorama, with distinctive features, significant age differences were not observed.

This is exactly what Craik's environmental support theory would predict. In an array of fairly indistinct black-and-white drawings, featureless boxes, or similar cue-sparse spaces, research participants must rely on their abilities to create memory traces with minimal help from the environment. However, if one provides recognizable, readily distinguishable cues (as in the case of Waddell and Rogoff's panorama), respondents have these "user-friendly" cues immediately at hand, and there is less reliance on self-initiated processing.

Under these conditions, older adults need not rely on relatively indistinct images, rendered worse by cognitive asynchrony. They can rely on more distinct, cue-rich representations from which greater numbers of relatively distinctive cues "survive" the relatively asynchronous processing characteristic of older adults. Consequently, performance is enhanced with distinctive arrays.

Systematic support for this idea was provided by a series of experiments (Sharps & Gollin, 1987b) which used table-sized and full-scale arrays of abstract shapes as task contexts. These arrays possessed the same layouts, but varied in the visual distinctiveness of their components, from simple black-and-white line-drawn "maps," to three-dimensional, multicolored wooden "models," to a large disused classroom in which the shapes were large and real. For example, a simple black-and-white circle, six inches in diameter, on the simplest plain map, was a bright yellow-painted six-inch circle on a "painted map," a six-inch high, six-inch wide unpigmented wooden cylinder on a "plain model," a six-inch high, six-inch wide bright yellow wooden cylinder on a "painted model," and a large yellow cable-spool in the disused classroom, the dimensions of which were to scale with those of the smaller arrays. In a variety of experimental frameworks using this basic task, respondents were typically asked to retain in memory the positions of thirty to forty common objects on these arrays over 120-second retention intervals.

It was repeatedly shown that increasing levels of visual distinctiveness, in terms of relief and color, decreased age differences in spatial memory to nonsignificance. With increased environmental support, age differences in spatial memory performance decreased, consistent with the environmental support hypothesis. It might also be noted that the more closely the level of distinctiveness of a given array approximated the rich visual diversity of the natural world in which young and older hunter-gatherers had to function, the less functional difference was observed between younger and older adults' spatial memory performance. This was not the result of scale or motor involvement, however; no differences in performance were observed between the classroom setting and the most distinctive table-sized arrays. The determining factor was the level of visual distinctiveness present in the cues to location.

So, one can support the internal representations created by older adults through the provision of visually distinctive environmental support. Most of the effect of environmental support on the recall

performance of older adults in this type of experimental task derives from conditions at encoding (Sharps & Martin, 1998).

These effects do not only extend to spatial memory. Similar data in the area of paired-associates learning (Sharps & Antonelli, 1997) were provided, in which the use of distinctive pictures enhanced the recall performance of the elders relative to that of the young. Interestingly, however, when a speed requirement was added to the task in a second experiment, this effect vanished: older adults performed at a lower level. This result, like the MR and spatial memory results discussed above, is consistent with the predictions of the cognitive asynchrony theory.

Evidence from Spatial Memory: Relational Importation Behavior

A variety of interesting extensions and limitations on these effects, based on task type, have been identified in the spatial memory realm (e.g., Arbuckle, Cooney, Milne & Melchior, 1994; Cherry & Park, 1993). However, the most important offshoot of this research for present purposes derived from work by Park, Cherry, Smith, and Lafronza (1990). This study, initially intended to be a replication of the spatial memory experiments of Sharps and Gollin (1987b, 1988), was in fact an interesting new study deviating in several ways from the original (Sharps, 1991; also see discussion in Craik & Jennings, 1992). Deviations included differences in instructions, the use of mobile rather than nonmobile structures, and the use of a transparent overlay that may have obscured some proximal cues in the array surface. The most interesting deviation, however, was Park et al.'s use of items that derived from readily identifiable categories. The Sharps and Gollin stimulus items were deliberately selected to avoid readily identifiable category inclusions: unrelated items such as a flower, a light bulb, and a paper clip were used. In contrast, thirty-two of the forty stimulus items Park et al. used derived from eight relatively homogeneous categories (e.g., kitchen things, hardware, smoking things). Using such stimuli, Park et al. failed to find unequal facilitation of older adult recall performance, and the performance of Park et al.'s older respondents was significantly poorer than that of the young across conditions of visual distinctiveness.

This result proved to be crucial for understanding the nature of verbal and imageric processing in spatial memory. In an unpublished experiment by Sharps and Gollin, in which a visually distinctive model "farm" and "beach" were constructed for use as arrays, and

toy farm implements and "beach things" (e.g., boat, starfish, towel) were used as stimulus items, an attempt was made to enhance still further the performance of older adults, by adding the mnemonic influence of categorical homogeneity of stimuli and context to the influence of visual distinctiveness observed in the previous model conditions. Surprisingly, the performance of the older adults relative to that of the young was significantly *depressed* in this work, a result similar to the lack of enhancement of older adult performance found by Park et al. with categorized stimuli.

The idea that the category factor was the source of the discrepancy was tested in a study (Sharps, 1991) in which young and older adults learned the locations of forty items on the plain map (which had previously produced age disparities in performance) and the painted model (which had produced age parity). Two sets of items were used in a between-subjects design. One set bore few if any recognizable relationships among the items, as was the case with the item sets used earlier by Sharps and Gollin. The other set was divided into ten categories of four items each, to give it a category structure similar to that of the stimulus set of Park et al. The results were as predicted: the uncategorized items replicated the results of Sharps and Gollin (1987b), providing a relative advantage for the recall performance of older adults. The categorized set, on the other hand, repeated the results of Park et al., providing no such advantage for elders.

So, it would appear that mixing visually distinctive cues with strong category cues is actively deleterious to the spatial memory of older adults. This result is highly counterintuitive, and leads to an obvious question: How can this be possible? The most parsimonious answer is suggested by the theoretical considerations discussed in chapter 1. The finding that the provision of two kinds of mnemonically valuable material, visually distinctive cues to location and category structure, actually *diminishes* elderly recall makes no sense if visual-spatial material and verbal material are processed at a relatively "ultimate" level in separate systems within the brain. At worst, they should not influence each other, and at best, they should synergize mnemonically in both young and older adults. However, if, as suggested above, *visual-spatial and verbal information in mind possess high levels of representational commonality at the ultimate level, diverging functionally primarily in response to experiential retrieval demand characteristics, then the resulting reliance on shared*

processing resources would be expected to produce exactly this pattern of results. The semantic, verbal, "relational' (Hunt & Einstein, 1981) information provided by category structure would be expected to undergo mutual interference with the item-specific visual-spatial information provided by the array, negating any mnemonic advantages for older adults, exactly as observed. Relational, semantic, category information would be "imported" (Sharps, 1997) into the task context, at the expense of the visually distinctive spatial details which would actually improve recall performance for both young and older adults.

Evidence from the Interaction of Spatial Memory and Free Recall

If this idea is correct, then a series of rather counterintuitive hypotheses, dealing with the effect of spatial encoding conditions on free recall performance, derives directly from it. The spatial memory results discussed thus far have come from the traditional realm of spatial memory dependent variables, specifically item *locations.* However, the considerations advanced thus far indicate that these effects should extend to item *identities.* The identity of an item is essentially, in Hunt and Einstein's terms, relational: we know *what* an item is, as opposed to *where* it is, by its relationship to other items of similar and contrasting types and categories. If the hypotheses advanced so far are accurate, the visually distinctive information inherent in the more distinctive arrays (such as the painted model and the disused classroom), and specific to given structures of those arrays, should meld relatively seamlessly with the relational information of item identities. The result should be that more distinctive contexts result in better recall of item identities, as well as in better recall of item locations.

Virtually any perspective on visual spatial memory other than the present set of considerations must predict the reverse. Visually distinctive cues should draw respondents' attention away from the specific items placed on the array, contributing to more effective location recall but certainly not to better recall of the items themselves.

Yet the counterintuitive result, consistent with the hypotheses driving the present research, is precisely what was observed. In experiments in which respondents were simply asked to recall, in list format, the items they had seen, rather than the locations of those items, more distinctive arrays resulted in *better* recall of item identities, not

worse, for both young and older adults. Also, as predicted and as was the case with location memory, older adults actually achieved parity of free recall with young adults in the more distinctive conditions (Sharps & Gollin, 1988); there was "unequal facilitation" of recall for the elderly, as the more visually salient characteristics of the more distinctive contexts compensated for the results of age-related cognitive asynchrony (Sharps, 1998).

An attentive reader may notice an apparent paradox in these results. It has been shown that relational information detracted from spatial memory, as cognitive resources were focused on relational rather than on spatial factors in the stimulus arrays. How then can item-specific spatial information be *contributing* to item memory? Shouldn't the negative effect of information importation go both ways?

The answer is no. There is no way that relational information can aid spatial recall. Where an item is located is entirely unrelated to what that item *is*. Focus on category structure must take the mind away from location. However, the examination of the visually distinctive details surrounding a given item in space may contribute directly to its identification precisely because such pictorial processing is detail-intensive: the spatial details become part and parcel of the memory per se. Verbal, category information, being relatively "chunked" and detail-sparse, does not become a part of the overall visual memory. Much more will be said on this topic later.

In addition to these findings, it was possible to test the cognitive asynchrony theory in three additional ways within this research framework. Three additional testable hypotheses concerning free recall in spatial memory flow directly from the theory:

1.   The free recall performance of older adults should be enhanced relative to that of young adults by spatial frameworks for recall, as opposed to nonspatial frameworks. This is consistent with the environmental support hypothesis of Craik (e.g., 1986, 1994): spatial cues to the locations of specific items should strengthen the traces representing those items in memory, as well as their locations, compensating at least to some degree for diminished processing resources in older adults, and resulting in diminished disparity between the recall performance of the two age groups.

2.   The free recall performance of older adults for item identities, as opposed to item locations, within this framework should also be enhanced relative to that of young adults by the presence of relational

(category-based) frameworks for recall within the spatial memory framework described above, especially in view of the relative preservation of relational processing systems across the adult life-span. The elderly should be able to take full mnemonic advantage of relational cues such as those provided by the category structure of stimulus sets to support item recall, as opposed to location recall, which was shown in the work described above (Sharps, 1991) to be actively diminished by the provision of relational information in the form of category structure.

3.   This effect of relational information in the form of category structure should be synergistic on item recall with the influence of spatial organization. Older adults should "import" the relational information of category structure into their representations of more-or-less distinctive spatial contexts. If, as suggested above, the two types of information are primarily distinguished by specific task demand characteristics, as opposed to actual representational characteristics, then a relatively "seamless" meld should be achieved, and item identity recall should be synergistically promoted by both types of cue.

Sharps, Foster, Martin, and Nunes (1999) provided a test of these three hypotheses in two experiments involving ninety young and older adults. The least distinctive map and the most distinctive model context from the work described above were used to anchor the continuum of contextual visual distinctiveness at low and high points, respectively. In the first experiment, respondents were exposed to forty categorically unrelated items either sequentially, one at a time in list format, or on one of the two contexts. Respondents were then asked to recall item identities.

The results were consistent with the hypotheses advanced. The performance level of older adults was significantly below that of the young in the list, nonspatial condition, but was at the same level as that of the young in both spatial support conditions. This expected unequal facilitation effect on free recall was consistent with the idea that the cues to location of the spatial arrays enhanced trace formation, so that elders did not have to rely as heavily on highly effortful self-initiated processing. Interestingly, even the map condition of this experiment produced age parity in performance. Apparently item recall, as opposed to location recall, can be enhanced in older adults by the mere presence of spatial cues, even less distinctive ones.

The second experiment repeated the procedures of the first, but with a stimulus item set derived from ten readily identifiable categories. The results of this experiment were also consistent with the

hypotheses advanced. Older adult performance did not differ from that of the young under any contextual condition, and list free recall performance for both age groups did not differ significantly from spatially supported performance. This showed that older adults were able to use relational information to enhance their recall to the level observed in young adults even in the absence of visuospatial support. Additional analyses of the results of these experiments were consistent with the hypothesis of a synergistic effect of spatial and relational support on the recall of older adults, as predicted (Sharps, Foster, Martin & Nunes, 1999).

Thus, the predictions advanced above, derived from cognitive asynchrony theory and from the representational considerations that devolve from that theory, were entirely supported by these results. In view of the complexity of these arguments, some of them, as seen, counterintuitive, let us recapitulate:

1.   The free recall performance of older adults was expected to be enhanced relative to that of the young by spatial frameworks for recall, consistent with environmental support theory (e.g., Craik, 1986, 1994). This was the result of the first experiment in this series; unequal facilitation of the free recall performance of older adults, above the level observed in the list condition, was observed in both spatial support conditions. This is consistent with the idea that spatial cues to the locations of specific items should strengthen the relevant traces, and that such cues will diminish the need for self-initiated processing, resulting in diminished disparity between the recall performance of the two age groups.

2.   The free recall performance of older adults within this framework was expected to be enhanced relative to that of young adults by the presence of relational (category-based) frameworks for recall. This was observed in the second experiment in this series; the use of related stimulus items obliterated any age-differential influence of spatial organization, resulting in age parity of performance across contextual conditions.

3.   It was also expected that when relational and visual-spatial frameworks were combined, so that visual detail could contribute to the relational realm (but *not* the reverse), recall performance would be enhanced, especially for older adults. This was observed across these experiments.

It should be noted that these synergistic effects were attenuated at longer retention intervals, as the distinction between initial pictorial

and relational characteristics blurred in representation over time, with a lower cognitive priority being placed on the maintenance of the relational character of the initial stimulus sets (see Sharps & Tindall, 1992). However, the evidence thus far, derived from studies of cognitive aging in the visuospatial realm, in MR, in spatial memory, and in item recall supported by spatial contexts, is consistent with the task-demand hypotheses suggested above. It is clear that spatial memory and spatial cognitive performance in young and older adults can be manipulated and interchanged to produce patterns of results ranging from massive age-related deficits to absolute parity of performance between young and older adults, depending upon predictable, systematic interactions of the task demands imposed and stimulus sets employed. The evidence is consistent with the idea that whatever the ultimate, presumably relatively unitary, nature of the representation of verbal/relational and pictorial/imageric stimuli, their experiential nature, as demonstrated by performance, is very much directly related to task demands, and to the predictable responses of young and older nervous systems to those demands. Divisions among information types can be effectively created or eradicated at will through the manipulation of task demands in these populations, consistent with the initial considerations driving this research. The evidence derived from the item-identity recall manipulations in particular suggests that these ideas and findings should prove relatively general, and should operate outside the spatial cognitive realm. This was the subject of the next series of experiments to be considered, experiments in the more general realm of nonspatial memory.

3

Minds through Time II:
What Aging and Nonspatial Cognition Reveal
about the Nature of Representation

A way of addressing the interaction of imageric and verbal representation in nonspatial realms was identified in studies (Sharps &
Gollin, 1986, April; Gollin & Sharps, 1988; Sharps & Tindall, 1992)
of the category superiority effect in free recall. The category superiority effect (CSE), also called the blocking effect (Gollin & Sharps,
1988) or the blocked-random effect (D'Agostino, 1969), is the well-
known effect of category organization on memory performance.
When items are presented "blocked" by category (members of one
category followed by members of another), they are remembered
better than when "unblocked" (members of several categories mixed
together) in a list format. We found, however, (Sharps & Gollin,
1986, April; Gollin & Sharps, 1988) that this effect only held for
verbal materials; the category superiority effect vanished for pictorial materials in young adults.

Why was this? The explanation lies in the information theory of
Hunt and Einstein (e.g., 1981), who, again, proposed a distinction
between "item-specific" and "relational" information. Item-specific
information includes details that are specific to a given item, in which
pictures are rich. Relational information includes category information, such as the functional or taxonomic category to which a given
group of stimulus items belongs.

These two types of information may prove redundant under certain processing conditions (Hunt & Einstein, 1981; Sharps & Tindall,
1992; see also Tulving, 1982). Item-specific information in memory
may replace relational information in terms of mnemonic value. The
gist of this argument, considered in depth in an earlier paper (Sharps
& Tindall, 1992), is this: pictures provide enough item-specific de-

tail to render relational information effectively redundant. When pictures are used in a CSE framework, the additional relational information provided by category organization provides no additional mnemonic effect, and there is therefore no CSE. However, when words are used as stimulus items, there is insufficient item-specific detail for optimal visual, item-specific processing. In the absence of such sufficient item-specific detail, the relational information provided by category organization is engaged, and a significant CSE is observed. Thus the CSE is explicable in terms of the interaction of item-specific and relational information within a given task, depending upon the types of stimulus materials employed.

Detailed evidence for these hypotheses is provided elsewhere (Sharps & Tindall, 1992; Sharps, Wilson-Leff & Price, 1995). For present purposes, the important point here is that the CSE paradigm provides a powerful method for answering a number of the questions raised above. A good departure point for this discussion lies in a counterintuitive question touched upon in our consideration of Sharps (1991), in which category information and visual spatial environmental support, both of which are salutary in isolation for the recall performance of older adults, combined to diminish, rather than enhance, spatial memory in elders. Let us reiterate what appears to be the best and most parsimonious explanation available for this effect.

As we've seen, there is evidence for diminished visual-spatial functioning with age, at least in part as a result of generalized slowing (although see Hertzog et al., 1993; Salthouse, 1995; Smith & Park, 1990, for evidence of task-demand dependency in this circumscribed area as well). However, semantic or relational processing is preserved relative to the processing of item-specific detail. Older adults probably use the more successful system when they can, using relational information (such as category membership) in memory, possibly at the expense of focus on visuo-spatial cues, whenever possible. If so, the spatial memory performance of older adults for categorized items should be relatively poor, exactly as shown in Park et al. (1990) and in the categorized condition of Sharps (1991). If a subject focuses on the category memberships of items, rather than on the item-specific information pertinent to their locations, his or her memory of those locations will of course diminish in proportion.

Where no such category memberships exist, however, older adults are forced to focus on visual-spatial cues. If those cues are suffi-

ciently distinctive, providing sufficient environmental support for recall, enhanced performance is achieved. This was observed in the uncategorized condition of Sharps (1991), and in all other extant work using uncategorized stimuli (e.g., Sharps & Gollin, 1987b, 1988; Sharps & Martin, 1998; Sharps, Martin, Foster & Handorf, 1999).

The hypothesis of age-related preferential utilization of relational information was specifically tested within the framework of a CSE study (Sharps, 1997). As stated, young adults do not yield significant CSEs with pictorial stimuli. However, if older adults do, in fact, use semantic information to compensate for diminished visual memory, we would expect significant CSEs from older adults even with pictorial materials.

This is exactly what was observed. Young and older adults were asked to recall forty items, ten from each of four categories, over a two-minute retention interval from a list-presentation format. Young adults yielded the typical pattern of results, strong significant CSEs for verbal items (printed nouns), and no CSEs at all for photographs of the items to which the nouns referred. Older adults, however, yielded strong CSEs for both pictures and words, as suggested.

But how do we know that older adults' diminished visual-spatial capacities, suggested to be based largely in the cognitive asynchrony of generalized slowing, really gave rise to this pattern? Granted that category information was used by older adults under conditions in which no such use was made by younger people, can we really make a strong claim that this is what actually happened?

The best way to provide a degree of certainty was to simulate this hypothetical age-related condition in young adults, and to see if their performance could be made to duplicate that of their elders. This was accomplished in two experiments (Sharps, Wilson-Leff & Price, 1995), actually published before the direct CSE comparison of young and older adults (Sharps, 1997). In most CSE studies, the author's group has used a five-second/item exposure time; this has been repeatedly shown to be more than ample for identification and processing of verbal and pictorial items by both young and older adults. In the Sharps, Wilson-Leff, and Price work, however, young adults were exposed to a four-category, forty-item CSE manipulation in which exposure times were systematically diminished. Respondents saw items for five seconds each, two seconds each, one second each, or 0.1s each. As predicted, with diminished exposure time, a significant CSE was observed for pictorial stimuli in young adults, dupli-

cating the performance of older adults at longer exposure times. In other words, when external representations were degraded artificially in young adults, a significant CSE "opened up" with decreased exposure time and consequent increased degradation, one which mimicked the CSE observed in older adults (Sharps, 1997), which results from the representational degradation of age-related cognitive asynchrony. With decreased exposure time, young adults behaved exactly in the manner of older adults, whose internal representations are proposed to be degraded naturally as a result of cognitive speed loss and the neural asynchrony which must result.

So, it appears that there is a complex interplay between pictorial, imageric, item-specific information, and relational, semantic, verbal information in the nonspatial as well as the spatial realm across the adult life span. The one type of information can compensate for lack of the other, depending upon task demands. Under other conditions, the one information type can *compete* with the other for what appear to be shared processing resources, also depending upon task demands. It should be noted that these effects are quite powerful. A clinical mnemonic system for older adults, based entirely on these principles and their application to maximize memory performance, was field-tested over multi-week periods with over forty community-dwelling older adult respondents. Everyday memory errors were reduced in this population by an average of 57-65 percent below baseline (Sharps & Price-Sharps, 1996). This effect was significantly, indeed several times, greater than any mnemonic effect ever reported for any pharmaceutical interventions. These findings testify to the power of these considerations in free-range field as well as laboratory conditions, and also to the potential for powerful applications that can be readily developed from these types of results.

Evidence from Aging and Nonspatial Memory: Specific Predictions

To reiterate briefly, cognitive asynchrony theory predicts that more complex data sets, such as those of pictures, will generally exhibit diminished processing with age in the manner suggested by Craik (e.g., 1986) and supported by Dror and Kosslyn (1994). This age-related diminution is suggested to result from the high level of item-specific information presented by a given picture; pictorial representations require a high order of synchronous processing to deal with their numerous item-specific components.

However, relational or semantic systems, which allow the subject to "chunk" (Miller, 1956) and automatize information, are predicted by the theory to be far less affected by the aging process. Chunked relational information relies less upon item-specific detail than does pictorial information (see Einstein & Hunt, 1980; Hunt & Einstein, 1981). Therefore, relational information can theoretically be processed in more holistic terms, in terms of fewer specific traces, and consequently with less involvement of cognitive resources, than can pictorial information. Since these resources are held to be negatively influenced by the gradual collective neural asynchrony of the aging process, the age-related difference in the processing of pictorial and relational information can readily be understood: the processing of relational information is less affected by asynchrony, and should therefore be generally easier than the processing of pictorial information in older adults (Sharps, 1997), although older adults can of course compensate for pictorial difficulties through the use of strong environmental support (e.g., Craik, 1986, 1992, 1994; Sharps & Gollin, 1987b, 1988; Sharps, 1991; Sharps & Antonelli, 1997; Sharps & Martin, 1998; Sharps, Foster, Martin & Nunes, 1999).

All of these findings combine to suggest very strongly that pictorial or imageric information, and verbal or semantic/relational information, may be interchanged, may behave like each other, or may be melded in either a salutary or deleterious manner, and that these processing characteristics vary in a complex but predictable manner with the age of the respondents. The pattern of results discussed thus far is at least consistent with the task-dependency concept of representation advanced above.

As was the case in the spatial realm, these considerations yield several specific predictive hypotheses which must be upheld if these ideas are, in fact, accurate, and which provide the potential for a strong test of their veracity. These hypotheses are as follows:

1.   In the presence of category information (which can be provided by category blocking), older adults should be able to attain levels of nonspatial list free recall comparable to those of young adults, given that the processing of relational information is suggested to be little diminished with advancing age.

2.   Older adults should yield a CSE with verbal materials comparable to that observed with young adults, again given that the processing of

relational information is suggested to be little diminished with advancing age.

3. Older adults should be able to use item-specific pictorial information to enhance their recall, as suggested by environmental support theory and by all of the author's spatial cognitive work to date.

4. Older adults should therefore yield a significant CSE with pictorial stimuli, unlike young adults who should not, as seen in earlier work (Sharps, 1997; see also Sharps, Wilson-Leff & Price, 1995).

5. Older adults should try harder to use category to structure their memory than do young adults, and should therefore cluster items by category more at retrieval than would be expected of young adults, again in view of the fact that the processing of relational information is suggested to be little diminished with advancing age, but that visual-spatial processing is more negatively influenced by the aging process.

6. It should also be possible to enhance the pictorial recall of elders to levels comparable with those of young adults through the provision of a prior framework for recall (e.g., Bransford & Johnson, 1973) which emphasizes the category structure of the stimulus set. This should be possible even under "unblocked" pictorial conditions, in view of the relative preservation of relational systems in older adults, and in view of the representational concepts suggested above.

7. In the presence of such a prior framework for recall, older adults should not yield a significant CSE, because the framework will obviate the need for relationally based mnemonic activity to compensate for age-related deficits.

Two experiments, involving two hundred and forty young and older adults, were conducted to test these hypotheses (Sharps, Martin, Nunes & Merrill, 1999). The first tested hypotheses 1 through 5 above, making use of a standard CSE task to address the hypotheses advanced. This experiment required young and older respondents to recall, in list format, sets of forty stimulus items. These sets each had ten items from each of four categories. Items were presented either as photographs of the items or as the printed names of those items (pictorial and verbal conditions, respectively), and were presented either blocked by category or unblocked. This relatively simple manipulation made it possible to test all five hypotheses. The results were in fact consistent with each:

1. *In the presence of strong category information (blocking) at encoding, older adults should be able to attain levels of recall comparable*

*to those of young adults, given that the processing of relational infor-
mation is suggested to be little diminished with advancing age.* This
hypothesis was supported: levels of recall under blocked conditions
did not differ between young and older adults.

2. *Older adults should yield a CSE with verbal materials comparable to
    that observed with young adults.* This was confirmed: both young and
    older adults yielded significant CSEs under these conditions.

3. *Older adults should be able to use item-specific pictorial information
    to enhance their recall.* This was confirmed: older adult recall of pic-
    torial materials did not differ significantly from that of the young.

4. *Older adults should, however, yield a significant CSE with pictorial
    stimuli, unlike young adults who should not.* This was also confirmed.

5. *Older adults should exhibit a greater degree of attempt to use cat-
    egory to structure their memory, and should therefore cluster items by
    category more at retrieval than would be expected of young adults.*
    This was confirmed; older adults exhibited significantly higher clus-
    tering of items by category than did young adults.

What about the sixth and seventh hypotheses advanced above?
All of the research discussed thus far, including the successful test
of the first five hypotheses in this series, indicates that provision of
relational information in the pictorial realm is a key factor in older
adult use of item-specific information to enhance recall. If so, it
should be possible to remove the CSE for elders under pictorial stimulus circumstances *through the provision of relational information
from some other source than stimulus blocking.* In short, older adults
should generate the same pattern of results typical of young adults,
with no CSE for pictorial stimuli, under conditions in which *relational information is available to govern recall for unblocked stimuli.*

An obvious source of such relational information is prior knowledge of the category structure from which items are to be derived.
Bransford and Johnson (1973) demonstrated that prior knowledge
of the semantic framework within which a piece of text could be
construed significantly enhanced recall for that text. Therefore, prior
frameworks for recall can provide for the enhancement of memory
performance, at least in young adults. Based on the theoretical considerations advanced above, little or no diminution of relational processing with age is suggested. It should therefore be possible to enhance the pictorial recall of elders to levels comparable with those

of young adults, and to remove the CSE from elders' recall of pictorial stimuli, through the provision of a prior framework for recall which emphasizes the category structure of the stimulus set to be remembered. Enhancement of older adult memory performance was expected to be possible even under "unblocked" pictorial conditions, again in view of the relative preservation of relational systems in older adults. In the presence of such a prior framework for recall, older adults were predicted *not* to yield a significant CSE, and to yield a pattern of recall virtually indistinguishable from that of young adults for both verbal and pictorial stimuli.

The second experiment in this series tested these hypotheses using materials and procedures identical to those of the first experiment, except in that prior to item presentation, the respondents were provided with the information that "these items come from four categories, animals, kitchen things, vehicles, and medical things" (the categories of item actually used), in order to provide a prior framework for recall.

The results were once again consistent with the hypotheses advanced. Although significant CSEs were obtained for verbal conditions for both young and older adults, there was no CSE for older adults under pictorial conditions, conforming to the predictions of Hypotheses 6 and 7. There was also a relative enhancement of older adult recall through the provision of a prior framework for recall that emphasized the category structure of the stimulus set. This prior framework resulted in no CSE for elders with pictorial materials, exactly as suggested.

Conclusions to this Point

Chapters 2 and 3 have presented an examination of specific aspects of cognitive aging related to the question of the segregation of information types. This examination has shown that, within the model system of the aging mind, different types of informational isolation and task dependency, the "walls" or barriers suggested in chapter 1 can and do exist as functional consequences of various types of cognitive task demands. Moreover, some light has been shed on the kinds of processes that can create these isolative functional barriers among different types of information which are processed by the relatively unitary electrochemical system of the brain. Furthermore, it has been shown that specific types of task demands can attenuate these barriers in terms of their functional effects, resulting in the

combination, synergy, or melding of different types of information, and creating predictable patterns of enhanced or diminished performance across the adult life span.

For individual human beings to make the kinds of intellectual errors described in chapter 1 (the sharks, the Mars orbiter, the faulty eyewitness testimony and the brick fort), functional discontinuities in cognitive processing must exist which make it possible to isolate information from decision contexts for which it is pertinent, or to isolate the information representing a given memory as it exists at encoding from the form of that memory at retrieval. Age-related declines in memory form a good model system for the initial consideration of these issues because memory does not decline with age as a global entity; different kinds of memory and memory declines are functionally isolated from one another, to different degrees, in the aging mind.

Age-related decline is localized in specific areas: the well-known cognitive speed loss, for example, and the visual-spatial deficit for which the results cited above, among others, provide evidence. In the realms of mental rotation, spatial memory, spatial support for nonspatial memory, and nonspatial recall, the findings discussed here indicate that support for visual-spatial processing may aid performance in the elderly, and that increased visual-spatial demand may result in performance decline. Incidentally, these findings also indicate that there may be considerable help for the cognitive processes of older adults, especially memory, in relatively simple, noninvasive manipulations of visual-spatial factors in materials to be remembered (Sharps & Price-Sharps, 1996).

However, the functional barriers which produce age-related differences in cognitive processes are neither anatomical nor based on differences in nature among information types. Rather, the isolative factors involved are based primarily on the cognitive asynchrony consequent on eugeric speed loss (e.g., Sharps, 1998), emerging effectively as epiphenomena from these bases. A wide variety of findings in visual cognition and aging may be unified in this manner under Birren's generalized slowing hypothesis, Craik's environmental support theory, and elements of Hunt and Einstein's information theory, which together form the bases of the cognitive asynchrony theory. With advancing age, adult cognition slows. The nature of this slowing results in necessarily asynchronous deterioration of specific processing elements. This means that older adults must place

greater reliance on environmental support for memory and related processes than do the young, especially in the processing of complex stimuli such as pictures and spatial layouts. When such support is forthcoming, older adults are capable of using it at a high level, in some instances to the degree that their recall performance is indistinguishable from that of college-aged control respondents. However, even when such support is readily available, older adults may refrain from using it. They may instead "import" relational information, the processing of which is relatively preserved through the course of the life span (since given elements of relational information require less cognitive synchrony and are hence less speed-intensive), into a given task to aid their memory. Regrettably, this tendency may result in a failure to exploit environmental support to the full extent possible, resulting in diminished memory performance. However, the present results demonstrate that under ideal conditions, these principles may be used to enhance the recall performance of older adults to very high degrees, effectively obliterating or at least attenuating the emergent barriers between different types and modalities of information processing in older adults. The basic principles advanced here may be extrapolated to the creation of extremely useful and economical memory aids for the use of older adults in everyday life. A clinical memory system developed from these principles (Sharps & Price-Sharps, 1996) has proven extremely effective, and constitutes both a point of support for the validity of this theoretical perspective and an immediate useful application of its extrapolation into the realm of applied psychology.

This work began with the idea that even though the ultimate representation of any given memory or thought must lie in neuronal activity, there are nevertheless functional barriers which can isolate the elements of cognitive processes from one another, both in memory and in the processes subsumed under the rubric of thinking. The most parsimonious and logical place to seek out these barriers, it was suggested, lies in the realm of demand characteristics and the responses of human beings of different organismic characteristics (in the present case, different ages) to those demand characteristics. The interaction of demand characteristics with the organismic capabilities which must respond to them is suggested to modify the relatively unitary representations which must be maintained at brain level into the imageric or verbal representations which are retrieved and processed at the experiential or psychological level.

Chapters 2 and 3 have summarized a program of research, the initial experiments of which began in 1984, which sought to examine these ideas in the realm of visual spatial and verbal processing. Cognitive aging was used in this program to develop a model system for these ideas. The results of this program of research have proven to be consistent with the representational considerations advanced here. Pictorial and verbal information have been shown to be predictably exchanged, interchanged, made mutually supportive, or made mutually deleterious to performance based on quality of representation across the adult life span, entirely in response to specific task demands. This work has proven to be useful in both the basic and applied areas (Sharps & Price-Sharps, 1996) of cognitive aging studies *per se*, and is certainly consistent with the more general representational concepts which are the primary focus of the present volume. With these demonstrations of both the feasibility and the predictive power of the concepts under consideration, it is time to address more purely representational issues, in an effort both to understand the full ramifications of these considerations and to work toward critical experiments which would test them more specifically.

4

The Processing of Auditory Imagery

Verbal, semantic, relational information, and pictorial, imageric, item-specific information, can be interchanged across the adult life span based on task demand, as was shown in the preceding chapters. Given these findings, the concept that, at some level, the one information type can literally *become* the other to some significant degree does not seem beyond the bounds of possibility. However, if verbal and pictorial information do share both a functional identity and a fund of processing resources at some level, it does not seem likely that these two types of information are processed in isolated, discrete systems which somehow exchange positions or provenances on demand. Rather, it seems more likely that there is a continuum of information expression, with purely verbal information processing or manifestation at one anchor point and purely pictorial manifestation at the other. If so, then there must be intermediate types, or levels, or continua of processing. What are they?

An obvious candidate for an intermediate type of information, which could serve in the building of a model system, lies in the realm of auditory imagery, the processing of sounds. One would expect this important dimension of human sensory and perceptual experience to have been thoroughly researched, so that the question of the intermediacy of auditory imagery could be addressed through the examination of prior studies. However, when one begins to examine the literature in this area (e.g., Crowder, 1993; Reisberg, 1992; McAdams & Bigand, 1993), one is faced with the interesting fact that auditory imagery *per se* has been very little addressed on either the memory or higher processing dimension. The auditory-imagery aspects of speech and language have been addressed very comprehensively, as has the role of auditory imagery in virtually every kind of music (e.g., Bigand, 1993; Halpern, 1992; Hubbard & Stoeckig, 1992). However, auditory imagery as such has been largely neglected

in the literature (Baddeley & Logie, 1992), and generally continues to be relatively ignored (e.g., Sharps & Pollitt, 1998). Cogent analyses of the auditory processing of words, phrases, sentences, musical notes, timbre, and pitch are all readily available; an understanding of the auditory images created by things themselves (e.g., the sound of a drill, the roar of a lion, the squeak of chalk on a chalkboard) is not.

Specialized anatomical structures for the processing of auditory images are of course known to exist, primarily in the temporal lobe in humans (e.g., Shepherd, 1994), just as specialized structures for the processing of visual information (primarily occipital) and verbal material (primarily frontal and temporal) also exist. This anatomical specialization might superficially lead to the conclusion that these types of information are in fact processed in isolation from one another. However, the existence of specialized anatomical structures for the perception and preliminary interpretation of these different types of information does not really imply functional processing isolation. In fact, given the need for the processing of fundamentally different types of energies derived from the visual and auditory realms; given the necessary conversion of light and mechanical energy, in vision and audition respectively, from the external environment into the electrochemical energy compatible with the brain; and given the specialized systems needed to convert both the spoken and written word into organized energetic systems which the brain can both process and organize, it would be remarkable if identifiable anatomical mechanisms for providing these relevant energetic pathways did not exist. The fact that different kinds of information in the external work make use of, and derive from, different types of physical energies would of course imply the existence of different kinds of neurological "tools" to cope with them, in a manner roughly analogous to the fact that electrical wiring in a house does not make use of pipes and valves, and that the plumbing system does not involve switches, wires and bulbs. The important question here is not one of initial intake and handling of stimulus energies, which of course require different types of systems for transformation and organization into the coding systems actually used by the brain. Rather, the question of concern here transcends the initial energetic vector of information. The central issue is one of how information, probably represented in a relatively interchangeable form at the ultimate level, is processed, modified and manifested at the experiential, or

proximate, level. The suggestion here, again, is that ultimately at the neurological level, verbal, auditory, and visual information possess some degree of interchangeability. However, the representational manifestation of these types of information at the experiential level should depend in part, probably in large part, on task demand characteristics.

It is of course certain that the relevant anatomical centers of the brain will play their roles in any given processing event. However, at least in passing, it should also be noted that the speed of neural conduction ranges from about forty to about one hundred and twenty meters per second, and that no given representational or experiential activity of the brain can in fact involve distances of over a few centimeters. In other words, there is plenty of neurological room for psychological representation, integration, and expression of information types, based both on their representational characteristics and on the task demands to which those characteristics are subjected; this is an area in which anatomy is most emphatically not destiny.

However, how solid is the concept of a processing continuum between the visual-spatial and verbal realms, on which continuum auditory imagery would hold an intermediate status? It has long been accepted that the mechanisms used to analyze auditory and visual inputs differ on many dimensions (e.g., Penney, 1975, 1989). Of this there is no real question. However, in recent years, it has also been shown that the processing of verbal and visual-spatial information, in the presence of other types of information in memory, involves complex interactions between task demands and stimulus characteristics, as discussed in detail in Chapters 2 and 3 (Sharps & Gollin, 1987a,b; Sharps & Gollin, 1988; Sharps, 1991; Sharps & Tindall, 1992; Sharps, 1998). It should be possible to modify and use the techniques employed in these experiments on the visual-spatial and verbal realms to address the question of non-musical non-linguistic auditory imagery along relevant experimental dimensions, and to determine the degree to which auditory imagery behaves in a similar or dissimilar manner to the processing characteristics of images and words.

The arguments developed here would suggest that auditory images should possess an intermediate character, partaking of the characteristics of both the verbal and visual/imageric ends of the continuum. Let us reflect, then, on the nature of that continuum. We have a fairly good idea of what we mean when we use the term

"verbal." But what are the characteristics of imagery? What do we actually know, at the functional, psychological level, of the characteristics of mental images at this point in the history of the field?

Visual and Auditory Images

Scholarly attention to mental images dates at least to the time of Aristotle. Visual mental imagery was used mnemonically by the ancient Greeks (Yates, 1966), and it was a major focus at the advent of scientific psychology, as well; Wundt (e.g., 1897) regarded an understanding of mental imagery as essential to the comprehension of the structural nature of consciousness. However, the study of mental imagery fell from favor during the first half of the twentieth century, with the advent of Watsonian behaviorism (e.g., Watson, 1913). Watson felt that the processes of thinking could most accurately and parsimoniously be considered without reference to the idea of images. Within his formulation, the subjective experience of imagery was somehow derived from subvocal verbal activity (Kosslyn, 1980: 455). This perspective dominated experimental psychology through the middle years of the twentieth century, and, not surprisingly, little attention was therefore devoted to the study of imagery during this period. However, with the rise of modern cognitive psychology in the latter half of the twentieth century, studies of visual imagery again began to emerge. Paivio, for example, in important work that will be discussed below, provided empirical evidence that imagery is a process that is functionally autonomous from, if interactive with, verbal cognition. Kosslyn and colleagues (e.g., Kosslyn, 1973; Kosslyn, Ball & Reiser, 1978) provided evidence that the scanning of a mental image requires real time, proportionate to the distance being scanned, in the same manner required by the scanning of a picture. The implication of these studies, that mental images maintained internal structural relations similar to those of physical pictures, strongly argued against a purely verbal idea of imagery. At around the same time, Shepard and colleagues (e.g., Shepard & Metzler, 1971), introduced the mental image rotation (also called the mental rotation) paradigm. In this task, as we saw above, abstract figures or alphanumeric characters are rendered in pairs of either identical items or stereoisomers. The twin items of each pair are rotated to different angles, and it is the task of the experimental subject to rotate them mentally into congruence, in order to determine whether the two items are the same or different (stereoisomers). Shepard and Metzler

(1971), and many other investigators who followed over the next two decades (see Sharps, 1990, for review) found that, in general, the reaction times of respondents in these experiments increased as a function of the angular rotation involved, again indicating a preservation of internal structural relations in mental images analogous to those of pictures and scenes in the real world. Thus, although visual images must of necessity arise from the basic neural activity of the brain, there is now no serious question that mental images do have a functional and experiential reality that wholly eclipses the possibility that images are an epiphenomenon of subvocal verbal activity (see Kosslyn, 1994). Images are real.

Does this mean that they are actually pictures themselves? No. This issue is treated in greater depth in chapter 5 below, but for the present, let us simply say that there are many differences between real-world pictures and mental images. For example, mental images lack the level of detail of pictures, and although images can be rotated and transformed in the mind, greater levels of intrinsic detail render this type of manipulation far more difficult for images than for pictures (Sharps, 1990: 330). There are other critical processing differences as well (e.g., Jolicoeur, Regehr, Smith & Smith, 1985; see chapter 5 below for full discussion).

Therefore, although images are real, functional, experiential things in the mind, they are at best roughly analogous to real-world pictures. This is of critical importance for the suggestions developed here. Pictures in the real world are relatively static things; they do not change of their own accord, or become blended with other real-world things such as songs and stories. They do not change with repeated examination, or lose details systematically with time. However, visual mental images are much more nebulous things, much more ethereal and changeable, and they do change in exactly these ways (e.g., Bartlett, 1932). Visual images are rough internal analogues of external visual events; but they are relatively plastic and changeable by comparison with external visual reality, and this character of mental images makes a variety of important cognitive processes, and errors in cognitive processes, possible.

Much less is known about auditory mental images as such. The vast majority of research on auditory cognition has concerned speech and language, which are of course by definition verbal processes, albeit auditorily mediated. A substantial amount of research has also been devoted to the psychology of music (e.g., Reisberg, 1992),

which must also be viewed as a special category or kind of auditory memory and thinking. Music has long been known to have its own logic and communicative functions (e.g., Wertheimer, 1910; Halpern, 1992). Therefore, although both music and language are of course crucially important subjects of study in their own rights, they provide a difficult ground for the testing of basic ideas about the fundamental nature of auditory imagery.

Auditory and visual imagery do have similarities, in that both reflect quasi-perceptual experiences of external stimuli. However, aspects of their basic organization are different; for example, visual images appeart to extend across and to be organized in a mental analogue of space, as shown by the work of Kosslyn and Shepard described above. Auditory images, on the other hand, extend and have their organization across time (Halpern, 1992: 3). For example, in a visual image of a cat, the two ears are separated in space, and the head may be to the left and the tail to the right. In an auditory images of the cat's meows, however, one meow or purr follows another in time, after the fashion of musical notes. This means that auditory images are even more ephemeral than are visual images, with a correspondingly greater reliance on the processes of working memory (Halpern, 1992). However, auditory images, like visual images, do encode somewhat degraded features of the external world into analogous representations. Where a visual image may have colors, textures, and spatial relations, an auditory image may have loudness and frequency (e.g., Intons-Peterson, 1992: 50-51), various qualitatively different features such as transformational invariants and differences in auditory grouping (McAdams, 1993), and organization in time. Little is known, however, about the degree to which the principles governing visual imagery extend to the auditory realm, in part because of the great methodological difficulties inherent in making such direct extrapolations (Halpern, 1992).

Nevertheless, when considering auditory and visual imagery together, we can say that both reflect internal rough analogues of external perceptual experience. Both depend upon remembered representations that are diminished in detail and in quality from their external analogues. Both rely upon specific types of features, and upon specific types of organization, with greater reliance on spatial organization in the case of visual representations and greater reliance on temporal organization in the auditory realm. But what about the interaction of visual and auditory imagery? Does auditory imagery

actually inhabit an intermediate level between verbal and the pictorial kinds of representations, as suggested above? Let us examine the evidence for this suggestion.

Evidence from Dual Coding

As mentioned above, visual imagery has long been known to have mnemonic value (e.g., Yates, 1966). Mental images and concrete visual representations yield higher levels of recall than verbal or more abstract items (e.g., Kirkpatrick, 1894; Paivio, 1971, 1986, 1990; Smith & Noble, 1965). The most parsimonious, and probably the most accepted, explanation of this phenomenon lies in Paivio's (e.g., 1990) dual coding theory. A word possesses only a verbal code, especially if it is an abstract word; a more concrete word has its verbal code and perhaps a shadowy internal representation of the image which that code is meant to represent. But an actual picture provides both verbal information (the respondent knows what the picture is supposed to represent) and the item-specific imageric data inherent in its pictorial nature. So, a picture of an item typically possesses full dual codes (verbal and imageric), whereas a verbal item does not. Thus recall is enhanced in the pictorial condition.

Where does auditory imagery stand in this situation? The considerations presented to this point in this volume indicate that an auditory image, like a visual image, should possess dual-coding characteristics. If a research participant hears the roar of a lion or the whine of a drill, that participant should have two codes to work with: the auditory image and the verbal label. Thus we would expect augmentation of memory for auditory imagery above memory for corresponding verbal materials, just as we would for visual pictures.

So, auditory and visual imagery should behave in the same way to enhance memory. This really says nothing about their shared processing characteristics, or any degree of identity between them-perhaps they are two different kinds of things which enhance memory, with no shared functional identity at all. However, a further prediction may be used to clarify this issue. If visual and auditory imagery are functionally separate things, then their combination in a given memory paradigm should result in higher recall than should the use of either alone-their independent mnemonic powers should synergize. If, however, they share processing resources in the brain,

thereby demonstrating some level of shared functional identity as suggested here, there should be interference between them; respondents' recall performance should not be enhanced farther by the use of both types of information than by either alone.

These hypotheses were tested in three experiments with one hundred and fifty college-aged respondents, who were asked to recall, in list format, items presented either as pictures (e.g., a picture of a lion, a picture of a drill), as auditory images (e.g., a recorded roar, a drill's whine), or as the printed names of the items. Other respondents received the visual and auditory images simultaneously (Sharps & Price, 1992).

The results of these experiments conformed precisely to the predictions given above. Both auditory and visual imagery enhanced recall significantly above the levels obtained with verbal stimuli. However, the combination of these two imagery types had no mnemonic effect beyond that of either alone, exactly as predicted.

What are we to make of these results? Clearly, both auditory and visual imagery enhance recall. Clearly, they also share processing resources. Whether these resources lie at the level of the need to divide attention, or at the level of memory consolidation, is not known, and may be a moot point—the precise level at which a given cognitive phenomenon ceases to lie in the realms of attention and perception and enters the suzerain of memory and reasoning has never been made clear, and the borders between these internal realms must be shadowy at best. The fact remains that auditory and visual imagery, two salutary mnemonic influences, do not synergize. The most logical and parsimonious explanation would seem to be that proposed above; that the two types of information share processing resources.

So, it has been demonstrated that auditory imagery is similar to visual imagery, and probably shares functional processing and processing resources, to some degree. This, of course, is consistent with the arguments developed to this point, and demonstrates the predicted relationship between auditory and visual imagery. However, these results say nothing about the intermediate character of auditory imageric information with reference to the verbal realm. In order to demonstrate the "verbal" as well as the "visual" character of auditory information, it was necessary to return to the study of the category superiority effect (CSE), utilized in the cognitive aging work described in the previous chapters.

Evidence from Studies of the Category Superiority Effect

Summarizing to this point, we know that visual imagery has mnemonic value (e.g., Kirkpatrick, 1894; Paivio, 1971, 1986; Paivio & Csapo, 1969; Paivio & Yuille, 1967, 1969; Smith & Noble, 1965; Yates, 1966). We know that a similar mnemonic value has been demonstrated for auditory imagery: the characteristic sounds made by items to be remembered (e.g., the roars of animals, the noise of power tools) were demonstrated to elevate recall scores above those obtained for purely verbal items, and to result in levels of recall similar to those obtained with pictures of the items (Sharps & Price, 1992). In addition, we know that, as predicted, the mnemonic value of auditory and visual imagery did not synergize.

What is the source of the memory advantage for auditory images? Characteristic sounds, termed "auditory images" for the sake of convenience, provide cues specific to the items to be remembered in the same way that visual images do. Pictures have visual features such as colors and contours; auditory images have specific features such as structural invariants, transformational invariants, macrotemporal and microtemporal properties (e.g., McAdams, 1993). Furthermore, just as the features of pictures may combine with verbal traces to enhance recall through dual coding (Paivio, 1971, 1986), the features of auditory images may also combine with verbal traces to result in a form of "dual coding," enhancing recall in the manner described by Sharps and Price (1992).

Again, when auditory images were combined with pictures, so that research participants were presented, for example, with a picture of a lion and simultaneously with the sound of its roar, recall was not enhanced beyond the level obtained with visual or auditory support alone. Auditory and visual detail did not result in additive enhancement of recall. This is strongly suggestive of shared resources, some level of functional identity, between the processing of auditory and pictorial stimuli. If the two types of images, auditory and pictorial, were processed independently, it would be anticipated that the synergistic effect of these two types of information would contribute to higher recall in combined auditory-pictorial conditions. As this was not the case, some functional interdependence in the processing of the two types of imagery appears a likely and parsimonious explanation of these results.

These findings raise an interesting and potentially important problem for current memory theory. Baddeley (e.g., 1986, 1990, 2001)

has provided what is probably the seminal theory of working memory. Baddeley holds that there is a central executive system, to which two "slave" systems are yoked: these are a phonological loop which deals with auditory stimuli such as music and speech, and a visual-spatial sketchpad (also called the visuo-spatial sketchpad; Baddeley, 1986) for processing visual materials and their spatial relations. Integration and processing of these kinds of information beyond the working memory level has not been characterized. However, it is reasonable to assume that what is happening in working memory will at least to some degree determine the character of representation and processing, or more precisely the character of representation and processing as interactive with task demands and task characteristics, at the deeper levels of consolidation, and storage. Thus is should be possible to address these characteristics of information processing at levels of processing that go beyond the bounds of working memory, and continue on through the consolidative activity of the brain.

What, then, should be the processing characteristics of nonverbal, nonmusical auditory images within Baddeley's framework, both in working memory and in the processing of the consolidated memory product at later memory stages? Clearly, one would anticipate phonological-loop processing of such stimuli, especially in light of evidence that such processing is the case for speech, complex musical passages, and even musical tones (e.g., Baddeley & Logie, 1992). However, as discussed above, there are apparently shared processing resources/functional identity characteristics of some degree between the processing of such auditory images and pictorial stimuli (Sharps & Price, 1992). Within which slave system does the processing of nonverbal, nonmusical auditory material take place? Either? Or both?

A possible solution to this question was suggested by Wilson and Emmorey (1997), who demonstrated the formation of a "visuospatial 'phonological loop'" in speakers of American Sign Language. In effect, it appears that the visual details of signs are translated into phonological codes for memory maintenance. Granted that ASL is analogous to verbal speech, whereas nonverbal, nonmusical auditory images are not. However, the ASL work does seem to indicate intermediate "gray areas" between the phonological loop and the visuospatial sketchpad, areas in which specific types of stimuli would partake of the processing characteristics of both systems, exactly as

suggested by the considerations advanced above. It seems probable that this is the most parsimonious explanation of the auditory imagery results obtained so far.

This idea was explored in a study of CSEs, which, again, are the well-known memory-enhancing effects of item presentation by category. As shown repeatedly (Sharps & Gollin, 1986; Gollin & Sharps, 1988; Sharps & Tindall, 1992; Sharps, 1997) and as discussed above, this effect is confined to verbal stimuli under most circumstances-strong CSEs for lists of verbal items are typically attenuated to nonsignificance when the equivalent pictorial items are used.

The CSE framework was ideally suited to an exploration of this domain, in that pictures obviously lie within the processing realm of the visuospatial sketchpad, whereas verbal stimulus items clearly fall into the realm of the phonological loop. It was therefore possible to examine the nature of nonverbal, nonmusical auditory images (hereafter simply termed "auditory images" for the sake of convenience) with reference to the two kinds of processing systems suggested by Baddeley. The primary hypothesis driving this research was that auditory images, given their auditory, phonological-loop-compatible characteristics, would yield significant CSEs, as would verbal items, even though auditory images have been demonstrated to have mnemonic powers similar to those of visual images, and to exhibit some degree of mutual intereference with the products of the visual-spatial sketchpad. As shown by Sharps and Price (1992), it was further expected that the overall level of recall of auditory images would significantly exceed that of verbal items. It was also expected that auditory image recall would achieve parity with recall of pictorial items, given the Sharps and Price (1992) results indicating process similarities between the visual and auditory image realms.

The CSE framework provided a way to determine whether or not auditory images actually have an intermediate character, partway between the visual and verbal ends of the processing continuum. If such an intermediate character exists, then auditory images should possess predictable processing characteristics in common with both visual and verbal items: auditory images were expected to yield significant CSEs like words, but to provide mnemonic advantages like pictures.

These hypotheses were tested with sixty college-aged participants (Sharps & Pollitt, 1998). For the sake of clarity, this experiment is described in some detail. A tape was made of forty common sounds

(e.g., a trumpet, a saw, a helicopter, a barking dog). The sound set contained ten sounds within each of four categories (animals, musical instruments, vehicles, and tools). (Only a few brief notes were included per musical instrument, sufficient to identify the instrument but not resulting in any melody or musical passage.) The sounds on this tape were presented "blocked" by category. All of the sounds used here were of course demonstrated to be readily identifiable.

A second tape presented these sounds in a random order, without reference to category (although no more than two sounds from the same category were ever allowed to occur sequentially). The two tapes, the categorized and the uncategorized, constituted the "blocked" and "unblocked" auditory image stimuli used in the study.

High-quality photographic slides of the items that made the sounds were obtained. Two sets were made, to provide blocked and unblocked pictorial stimuli. Finally, high-quality slides of the names of these items were made for the blocked and unblocked verbal stimulus conditions of the study. Items were presented sequentially to respondents, using, of course, a between-subjects format.

The results were exactly as anticipated. Auditory images and pictorial images were not recalled at significantly different levels, consistent with previous work (Sharps & Price, 1992). However, recall in both of these conditions was at a level significantly higher than that obtained with verbal items; in other words, auditory and visual imagery provided statistically identical levels of mnemonic advantage over purely verbal materials, presumably as a result of dual coding (Paivio, 1990), exactly as predicted. Blocking by category resulted in higher recall than did the unblocked stimulus conditions, also as predicted, but only with verbal *and with auditory stimuli.* Visual stimuli did not yield a CSE, as has been repeatedly demonstrated (e.g., Sharps & Tindall, 1992). So, auditory imagery and verbal materials possessed the predicted shared relationship with reference to the generation of CSEs, the use of semantic category information to support recall.

To reiterate, auditory imagery had mnemonic value similar to that of visual imagery. Conditions in which participants were exposed to auditory or to pictorial stimuli produced recall at about the same levels, significantly above the level observed for verbal items. Thus the idea of functional similarity and shared processing resources between pictorial and auditory items again received support. However, as suggested, the processing of auditory image items was also

similar to that of verbal items: significant CSEs appeared for both auditory image and verbal stimuli in this study, whereas no such effect was evident for pictorial materials.

Although these results do not, of course, make it possible to specify the ultimate mechanisms of visual or auditory image processing or representation, they do suggest that the processing of nonverbal nonmusical auditory imagery has a character intermediate between those of visual images and verbal items. Auditory images are similar to verbal items in being influenced by category manipulations such as blocking or its absence, consistent with the idea that auditory images may be identified functionally with the phonological loop in working memory at least. At the same time, the mnemonic character-istics of auditory images are more similar to those of pictorial materials. In light of Wilson and Emmorey's (1997) demonstration that the pro-cessing characteristics of American Sign Language, a visual communi-cation system, are such that ASL signs appear to operate within the visuospatial sketchpad system of working memory, these findings in-dicate that there are stimulus materials and situations which have an intermediate character. Together with Wilson and Emmorey's (1997) result, and that of Sharps and Price (1992), these findings provide fairly strong evidence that auditory images require processing re-sources from both the visual-spatial and phonological systems.

Does this mean that the visuospatial sketchpad and phonological loop are the same? Are these results inconsistent with current work-ing memory theory? Emphatically not. There is strong evidence that the visuospatial sketchpad and the phonological loop are function-ally distinguishable systems (e.g., Baddeley & Logie, 1992; Baddeley, 1986, 1990, 2001). What the present research and considerations indicate is that the two systems may be required to work synergisti-cally and with overlap in some stimulus situations, *depending, once again, upon task demand characteristics.* The most likely sets of task demands in which these processing characteristics are likely to manifest themselves are visual-spatial situations with inherent se-mantic meaning (Wilson & Emmorey, 1997) and auditory situations with inherently high levels of nonsemantic detail (Sharps & Price, 1992; Sharps, Price, and Bence, 1996; Sharps & Pollitt, 1998). So far, the idea of a continuum of processing, which exhibits divisions among information types depending upon the interactions of task demands with representational characteristics and organismic char-acteristics such as age, is consistent with the data.

Specific Predictions of the Effects of Auditory Imagery:
The Nature of the Primacy Effect

In previous experiments addressing only verbal and visual materials, without reference to auditory imagery, CSEs which were present and significant for verbal items disappeared for their pictorial counterparts. These effects were principally due to elevation of scores for ungrouped pictures to the same levels observed with grouped pictures. Analyses for ceiling effects, incidentally, were negative; the loss of CSEs for pictures in these experiments reflected true relative score elevations without ceiling effects.

Let us return to the distinction between item-specific and relational information proposed by Hunt and Einstein (Einstein & Hunt, 1980; Hunt & Einstein, 1981) to provide additional perspective within which this stimulus dependency may be explained. Item-specific information, such as idiosyncratic visual detail, is of course specific to given items, rather than being shared among items in a given list to be recalled. In contrast, relational information, such as membership in taxonomic or functional categories, may be shared in common among the items of a given list.

Pictorial stimuli of course contain much item-specific information, as well as relational information such as category membership. A picture of an elephant, for example, is identifiable as a member of the category of elephants (relational information), but it also has idiosyncratic detail (item-specific information) specific to that particular elephant. This, of course, is the basis of the mnemonic advantage provided by dual coding (e.g., Paivio, 1990). Verbal items, in contrast, are more "relational" in nature; the word "elephant" denotes an abstract member of the category of elephants, not any specific individual elephant. In studies of the CSE cited above (e.g., Sharps & Gollin, 1986; Gollin & Sharps, 1988; Sharps & Tindall, 1992), pictorial stimuli, rich in item-specific information, rendered the added mnemonic boost of relational characteristics (category information) unnecessary to achieve optimum recall, and CSEs were not observed. In contrast, when the items to be remembered were verbal, category information became more important and significant CSEs resulted. Thus many of the effects, discussed above, which derived from the pictorial, imageric, visual-spatial realm, probably derived from the rich levels of item-specific information inherent in pictorial information. Those that derived from the verbal, semantic

realm, on the other hand, probably came from the predominantly relational nature of verbal stimuli (Sharps & Tindall, 1992). The nature of auditory imagery is suggested to partake of both the item-specific and relational realms (Sharps & Price, 1992; Sharps, Price & Bence, 1996; Sharps & Pollitt, 1998).

These considerations may be profitably applied to the study of a familiar effect in experimental psychology, but one which still presents enduring mysteries: the serial position curve, in particular the primacy effect.

The reason to bring the study of auditory imagery to bear on the primacy effect was twofold: to shed some light on the still rather mysterious nature of the effect, and to test the present considerations in yet another realm in which data consistent with a specific, nonintuitive hypothesis must be obtained if the theoretical perspectives advanced here are accurate. The intent was to provide the most stringent tests of these perspectives possible, in as many experimental realms as possible.

The working hypothesis here was that primacy effects must be considered "relational" in nature: primacy effects result from the position of items within a given list, from their *relationship*, in terms of temporal order, with the other items to be remembered. This is not, of course, to say that the type of relationship to be found in temporal order is necessarily analogous to interitem relationships by category. However, in terms of Hunt and Einstein's (e.g., 1981) distinction, information derived from relationships based on temporal order certainly possesses a more relational than item-specific character. Granting this, and in light of the CSE results discussed above, we would therefore expect that strong item-specific information, such as that provided by pictorial stimuli, would attenuate primacy effects just as it has been shown to attenuate category superiority effects.

Why focus only on the primacy effect, rather than on both ends of the serial position curve? These experiments treated primacy effects, rather than recency effects, because of the difference in the probable sources of these phenomena. Recency effects have typically been thought to result from the continued presence in short-term memory of the most recent items of a given list. However, this explanation has encountered contradictory evidence, notably in the existence of long-term memory recency effects (e.g., Baddeley & Hitch, 1977). Baddeley and Hitch (1993) argue convincingly that recency may better be construed as resulting from the relative ease

of discrimination of more recent stimuli, an activity that obviously places a premium on item-specific information. Thus a recency effect, while presumably resulting from relational factors, is also held to involve item-specific factors at a process level. This would pose a serious problem in the discrimination of item-specific from relational influences on recall for any given recency item.

The primacy effect, on the other hand, is generally regarded as a matter of rehearsal, not of discriminative ability; the longer a given item has been in the memory system, the more opportunity for rehearsal it has undergone, and the better its consequent recall (e.g., Bruce & Papay, 1970; Crowder, 1976). Although other processes may be involved in the primacy effect, rehearsal has generally been shown to be the dominant determinant (e.g., Wixted & McDowell, 1989). There is evidence for this in the finding that, in the presence of instructions to rehearse each item in a list equally often, the primacy effect disappears (Fischler, Rundus, & Atkinson, 1970; also see Rundus, 1971). This indicates that the primacy effect depends on the temporal position of the initial items learned relative to later items in the list, a relational type of information. The primacy effect is therefore definable as relational in nature.

This is not, of course, to suggest that items appearing early in a given list are more strongly related to one another than items appearing later in the list. Rather, the type of relational information suggested is the relationship of the items to the list as a whole, specifically to their relative position in that list. The type of relationship discussed here is not interitem, but the more abstract relationship of item to temporal item position. However, if the definition of "relational" information includes this type of relationship, and if primacy effects therefore represent a type of relational information, they should be attenuated or suppressed by the use of pictorial stimulus items, because pictorial items are rich in visual, item-specific detail. This was the primary hypothesis driving the research reported here (Sharps, Price & Bence, 1996).

The effect of auditory imagery, as well as that of visual imagery, was also tested in the following experiments, to ascertain whether the intermediate character of auditory imagery, suggested by the experiments cited above, can be predictably manipulated within the primacy effect research framework. The type of auditory input used here, just as in the studies already cited, consisted of the characteristic sounds made by stimulus items.

Functional commonalities between auditory and visual imagery have been demonstrated, as discussed above. However, consistent with the idea of an intermediate character for auditory imagery, there are many functional differences as well, which manifest themselves under different conditions of task demand. Auditory input is held longer than visual information in sensory memory (Crowder & Morton, 1969), and recency effects are stronger for auditory than for visual information, although primacy effects are not (Corballis, 1966; Laughery & Pinkus, 1966; Madigan, 1971; Murray & Roberts, 1968; Routh, 1971). Also, characteristic sounds lack much of the item-specific detail that would be expected to suppress primacy effects in the case of visual stimuli. We would therefore anticipate that the use of auditory stimuli, in contrast to visual stimuli, would produce little or no attenuation of the primacy effect, as do verbal items that possess even lower levels of item-specific detail, and are presumed to be processed phonologically. In other words, in this instance, auditory images are expected to behave more like words than like pictures. The relative lack of item-specific detail in both verbal and auditory-image items should create a task demand situation which is relatively dependent upon relational considerations, and the primacy effect, suggested above to be primarily a relational phenomenon, should manifest itself with both verbal and auditory-image stimuli.

What about attenuation of the primacy effect by pictorial stimuli? The research literature on primacy effects for pictorial stimuli is mainly limited to recognition studies. Phillips and Christie (1977) found no primacy effects in recognition memory for visual patterns. Rose (1976) identified evidence for modest primacy effects in recognition memory for line drawings, but also believed that the possibility of initial output interference effects rendered this conclusion suspect. There appear to be very little data available on pictorial list recall, as opposed to recognition. Therefore, as in previous studies of the category superiority effect, the first experiment in the series to be described focused on primacy effects in free recall. Photographs of items, the recorded characteristic sounds made by those items, and the printed verbal names of those items once again constituted the stimulus sets used. Seventy college-aged adults participated in this study, which used forty stimulus items of each type. The items were semantically unrelated, to prevent any forms of contaminative clustering that might arise from category commonality.

Respondents were presented with the items from one of the three stimulus sets, or combined in all possible simultaneous permutations (auditory images + words, auditory images + photographs, auditory images + words + photographs, etc.) in list format, and were then asked to recall the items. The experiment of course used a between-subjects design.

Some consideration of measurement methods in this study is in order here. The measurement of primacy effects is complex and controversial (see Baddeley, 1986; Baddeley & Hitch, 1977, 1993; Fischler, Rundus & Atkinson, 1970; Rundus, 1971). The venerable technique of finding list recall asymptote and then comparing performance on the first few items with asymptotic performance presented problems in earlier CSE work with "real world" stimuli, such as pictures of actual objects; the range of recall for specific items within lists has often proven to be large, and may sometimes result in inaccurate and spuriously high estimates of asymptote. Moreover, there is no consensus on what portion of a given list may be reliably taken as representing the "first few" items within any given type of experimental task. Therefore, all of these difficulties were circumvented through the simple expedient of quartile analysis. The four quartiles of each stimulus list condition were generated by dividing the list into four equal parts by rank order of presentation. Thus the first ten items represented the first quartile, the next ten the second, and so on. Although such a technique would obviously be inappropriate for the precise measurement of primacy effects within conditions, it provided a relatively clear and robust way of assessing the simple existence or relative absence of such effects *between* conditions, the purpose of the study.

The results of this experiment were consistent with the hypotheses advanced. It was suggested that verbal and auditory input would be associated with significant primacy effects, but that pictorial input would not, because only pictorial input would provide sufficient item-specific detail to render the relational information provided by list order moot. This was confirmed; a significant primacy effect was discerned both for verbal and auditory stimuli, but not for any condition involving visual stimuli, although it is interesting to note that some nonsignificant indication of a primacy effect was observed in the "auditory + visual" condition, consistent with the idea of shared processing resources advanced by Sharps and Price (1992). It should also be noted, consistent again with the shared functional identity

concept, that the primacy effect achieved with auditory images alone was considerably smaller than that obtained with purely verbal stimuli (Sharps, Price & Bence, 1996).

So, when strong item-specific information was provided, through the use of item photographs, the primacy effect was suppressed to a nonsignificant level. However, when photographs were not used, and item-specific information was therefore relatively unavailable, significant primacy effects were observed, both for verbal and auditory stimuli. These findings were consistent with the hypothesis that the primacy effect could be attenuated by strong item-specific information, and may therefore be interpreted, at least within the present research framework, in relational terms. Also, auditory input, like verbal information, resulted in a primacy effect, rather than in the attenuation of the primacy effect observed with visual stimuli. This result was also consistent with the hypothesis advanced, of shared processing resources and similar functional characteristics between the auditory-imagery and verbal realms, as well as between the realms of auditory and visual imagery.

Similar results were obtained in an experiment (Sharps, Price & Bence, 1996) in which instructions to use internal mental visual imagery were utilized. In the first experiment in this series, the provision of item-specific information attenuated the primacy effect, principally through elevation of mid-list recall. This second experiment evaluated the question of whether a similar result could be attained through the use of internal mental imagery alone, as opposed to the presence of strong potential for imagery inherent in pictorial items themselves. This internal-visual-imagery experiment was rooted in earlier work by Bower (1970), who instructed respondents to form visual images in several visual stimulus conditions. Bower found that respondents tended to generate visual pictorial images even in the absence of actual stimulus pictures if instructed to do so.

These images, while presumably neither as detailed nor as maintainable as those derived from actual pictures, must of course provide a form of item-specific information (e.g., Paivio, 1986). Thus if a respondent were asked to envision specific items, as in the work of Bower (1970), the resultant images would be expected to have a mnemonic function analogous to that of the item-specific visual information provided by an actual picture. It was therefore expected that imagery instructions would serve to attenuate primacy effects for printed word stimuli, as the item-specific informa-

tion inherent in the internal images overwhelmed the use of the relational information derived from the list order of the stimulus items.

This effect was not anticipated for auditory-input stimuli, however. Sharps and Price (1992) showed that although both auditory and visual input had mnemonic power, combining sounds with pictures provided no further mnemonic value beyond what was accomplished with either alone. This, of course, implies that auditory and visual imagery share processing systems at some level, so that possible synergistic advantage of the two types of imagery together may be offset by their mutual depletion of the same cognitive resources.

If this is indeed the case, we would expect that the processing of auditory-input stimuli might actually interfere with the processing of internally-generated visual images, resulting in weak item-specific information products which would be unable to elevate midlist recall to the degree that significant attenuation of the primacy effect would be observed. Therefore a significant primacy effect would be expected in auditory input conditions, even in the presence of imagery instructions.

This experiment made use of eighty college-aged participants, and used the same materials and effectively the same procedures as the first experiment in this series. Half of the participants in each stimulus condition received the procedure exactly as administered in the first experiment. The other half, however, were first instructed to generate visual images to correspond with the verbal, auditory, or visual stimulus items that they heard or saw. This made it possible to test the degree to which internal visual mental imagery would tend to diminish primacy effects for verbal stimuli, or would tend to provide mutual interference with the influence of auditory stimuli. This in turn, of course, also provided an additional test of the intermediate character of auditory imagery.

The results of this experiment were consistent with the hypotheses advanced. Verbal materials yielded a significant primacy effect without imagery instructions, but the primacy effect was attenuated to nonsignificance by the use of imagery instructions, which presumably enhanced the mnemonic quality of internal representations through the internal generation of additional item-specific detail. Also as expected, no conditions involving pictorial stimuli resulted in significant primacy effects: imagery instructions could not add item-

specific detail to the already concrete levels of detail provided, so to speak, by the real things. Auditory stimuli without imagery instructions resulted in a significant primacy effect, in a manner analogous to verbal materials. However, interestingly and as suggested by the work of Sharps and Price (1992), the addition of imagery instructions to auditory input also resulted in a significant primacy effect, consistent with the idea of competition for shared processing resources between the processing of auditory data and the processing of visual-spatial information, in this case the processing of internally generated visual-spatial information.

So, and to summarize, pictorial stimuli may suppress the primacy effect, even in the presence of auditory input, but neither auditory nor purely verbal stimuli do so. Significant primacy effects are created, however, when either auditory or verbal materials are used in the absence of pictorial stimuli, indicating shared characteristics between the auditory and verbal realm. Instructions to create internal visual images have different effects for verbal and auditory stimuli, consistent with the idea that some characteristics of auditory processing have more in common with the visual-spatial realm. In other words, the contention that auditory imagery bears an intermediate character on a continuum between purely visual (and item-specific) and purely verbal (and relational) types of information was entirely supported in these experiments (Sharps & Price, 1992; Sharps, Price & Bence, 1996; Sharps & Pollitt, 1998).

Conclusions Drawn from this Research to this Point

The results of the experiments described in chapters 2, 3, and 4 provide strong support for the axiomatic considerations described in the first chapter, and for the hypothetical nature of representation suggested by the axioms. Let us briefly reconsider those axioms, and the new information derived from them, as we move toward an attempt to unify all of these considerations in a synthetic theory of the relevant aspects of information processing.

Axiom I. *Information can be available in memory and yet have no effect on a given decision.* Even if information is known, it may not influence a decision for which it would be relevant. Bad decisions are not only made in ignorance. Sometimes they are made even when information that should have prevented those decisions is known to the subject.

Axiom II. *There must be divisions, inherent in information processing, between different kinds of information (e.g., pictorial and verbal information), divisions which allow different types of information to be processed and to exist in relative isolation from one another.* If a decision can be made in ignorance of relevant information which is nevertheless known to the individual involved, this means that although the relevant information is present in memory, it is not present in the immediate computational environment of the decision in question. This implies the existence of separable processing systems, in which these cognitive processes can proceed in isolation from one another. In effect, there is a strong suggestion of some sort of multistore processing system, with some sort of isolative barriers, sometimes breachable and sometimes not, dividing the relevant information within different internal cognitive environments. The bad decision or faulty cognitive processing is going on in one metaphorical cognitive space, and the necessary information which would prevent the bad decision or outcome is irrelevant because it is resident, somehow, in another. Multistore models are of course known in psychology (e.g., Atkinson and Schiffrin, 1968; Paivio, 1986, 1990; Baddeley, 1986), so this is certainly empirically possible as well as logically necessary.

Axiom III. Even so, *the ultimate nature of the representation of both kinds of information, indeed of all kinds of information, must lie in the electrochemical activity of the brain's neurons.* So, there is a difficulty. Images and words are experienced differently by the given subject. Working memory and long-term memory have different functional characteristics. Yet ultimately they must be the same *kind* of information across anatomical regions of the brain itself, resident in the electrochemical activity of the brain's neurons.

Superficially, this may not seem like much of a problem. After all, the necessary neural substrates may exist separately, with anatomical barriers between them. Specialized anatomical structures for the processing of auditory images are known, primarily in the temporal lobe in humans (e.g., Shepherd, 1994). There are also specialized structures for visual processing in the occipital lobe. Verbal material is handled in several special structures, placed exactly where one would expect: Broca's area, the center of speech production, is located in the frontal lobe very near to the motor strip which controls the motions of the muscles involved in speech; Wernicke's area, re-

sponsible for speech reception, is located near the auditory cortex; and all the relevant structures are relatively close together in the left hemisphere in the vast majority of human adults. So, perhaps there is no conflict: these types of information, visual, auditory, and verbal, are anatomically separated, and the necessary barriers may be neuroanatomical ones. When a given activity (such as reading) requires several of these abilities at once, the relevant anatomical regions may simply be activated independently.

Unfortunately, this superficially satisfactory story begins to break down almost immediately. For one thing, all of the senses, except for olfaction, route their input to the thalamus for redistribution to the relevant brain centers. Anatomical distinctiveness of representation by input type at the deeper levels is not, so far as is known at this time, retained. As noted above, given the fact that vision is dependent upon light energy, and hearing upon the mechanical energy of sound, it would be very unlikely, not to say impossible, not to have specialized systems for dealing with the physical characteristics of these different types of energies.

The fact remains that, at base, one is dealing with a relatively unitary type of electrochemical cellular activity as the basis of representation at the cellular level, a type of activity capable of traversing the diameter of the brain in a minute fraction of a single second. Anatomical barriers, in short, if they exist at all, would have to be extraordinarily sturdy, and they would have to function in a very odd manner, to be the basis of information isolation in the brain. A different source of such barriers is much more likely.

"Axiom" (Thesis) IV. *Given all of these considerations, information must have both an ultimate and a proximate nature.* In other words, information must have a nature that lies along a continuum from the ultimate level of representation in the neuroelectrochemical activity of the brain to the experiential manifestation at the "proximate" level of behavior.

If so, then something must cause the nature of that manifestation, the nature of the conversion of an ultimate electrochemical representation into a memory of a sentence, or of a picture, of a sound, or of an idea. This leads to the question of precisely what determines the nature of the behavioral, proximate level of representation. The hypothetical answer to that question is that *it is the demand characteristics of the given cognitive task which predominantly determine*

the proximate, or experiential, nature of the information in question. These demand characteristics, of course, are interactive with the abilities which given human organisms bring to the cognitive task context, abilities which will vary with age, as demonstrated above, and presumably with other organismic and learned characteristics as well.

Does the research cited thus far support or provide consistency with these propositions? Yes. Young adults differ from older adults in that pictorial materials are relatively harder for older adults to process, by comparison with young adults, than are verbal materials, which would seem to imply isolative functional barriers between the processing of verbal and imageric information, barriers whose nature changes with age. Yet it was shown in a number of experiments, in both the spatial and nonspatial memory realms, that these barriers, at the proximate level, are the function of task demands. These demands interact with specific characteristics of the aging process, specifically with the consequences of the cognitive asynchrony that results from eugeric speed loss (Sharps, 1998).

These interactions, however, can be modified. Through the provision of environmental support, age differences in visual-spatial processing were eradicated in a variety of experiments. Through the alteration of speed requirements and stimulus characteristics in CSE frameworks, verbal information was imported by older adults to support pictorial memory in a way that differed entirely from the processing characteristics of young adults, until speed-related task demands were imposed which caused young adults to engage in exactly the same type of barrier-breaching "relational importation behavior" (see Sharps, 1997).

What about the basic division between visual and verbal material without regard to age? Experiments focused on auditory imagery have shown that the characteristic sounds made by given items in the real world lie between the visual and the verbal realms in terms of processing characteristics. This does not suggest two discrete systems. Rather, the results of these studies strongly suggest a continuum, on which the verbal or auditory or visual character of a memory is manifested according to, once again, the demand characteristics of the given situation. Furthermore, it appears that it is the level of relational and/or item-specific processing required in a given task that provides much of this evident distinction.

A few years ago, the story of the phenomena addressed to this point in this volume might have run something like this: "Old people have bad memory for some reason, probably because their brains deteriorate in different ways, and they're especially bad with visual memories when compared with young people. Visual and verbal memories are processed separately, so maybe there is something wrong with old people's ability to hook the components of these separate systems together. Therefore, they can't do dual coding as well as they used to, and so they don't remember pictures as well."

Now, however, we're prepared to offer a somewhat simpler, more parsimonious, and at the same time more complete picture: Although information is initially encoded with reference to its energetic characteristics (radiant, mechanical, etc.) by specialized neurological systems, the ultimate representation, when made manifest at the proximate, experiential level, is less a result of the initial stimulus type than it is of the demand characteristics to which that information is responding in any given cognitive task situation. However, there is a continuum of representation, rather than a series of discrete types, with verbal and visual representation marking two anchor points on this continuum, and with auditory imagery possessing intermediate characteristics between them. The more visual or visual-spatial a representation is, the more one must rely upon item-specific features to process it. More verbal individual items offer fewer item-specific characteristics, and so the respondent must rely upon relational characteristics, such as the category membership of the given item, in processing such items. (Please note that this refers to the individual verbal item, rather than the verbal item embedded in related text; this topic will be considered below.)

These are the reasons why older adults have more trouble with memories that involve greater degrees and levels of pictorial processing. The generalized speed loss experienced by aging nervous systems results in a cognitive asynchrony that makes it more difficult to process, in the necessary synchronous, often simultaneous manner, the item-specific characteristics which define the pictorial item. Individual verbal items, which require less synchrony due to their relational character, may prove somewhat easier for older adults under many cognitive task circumstances. This is because verbal items may pack a great deal of meaning into a given concept, effectively providing a verbal label for a variety of items that may be subsumed under that label (Lakoff, 1987), without the requirement

of item-specific analysis of the several items included. Verbal material may therefore provide relational information to shore up or support diminished visual spatial abilities.

If this line of reasoning is valid, then the nature of experiential representation relies a great deal upon whether a given information processing event is more concerned with item-specific or with relational aspects of the initial representation. This is not, of course, to say that whether one saw an elephant or read the word "elephant" is irrelevant; quite the contrary. One cannot veridically remember item-specific characteristics (e.g., yellowed or chipped tusks, ragged or symmetrical ears) if one never saw them in the first place (although, especially significantly in the case of eyewitness identification proceedings, one can always make them up, either by design or inadvertently as we've seen above). However, although of course at the ultimate level verbal and visual representations are probably not identical, the argument here is that they share sufficient characteristics for confusions to occur, especially if the demand characteristics of the given cognitive task involving those representations promote such confusion. And furthermore, *it is the item-specific and/or relational nature of both the representation and the task demand* which are suggested to be responsible for the final, experiential information product or performance produced by a given respondent in a given cognitive situation.

With this as background, it is now possible to suggest and test a synthetic theory of the nature of representation. It must be admitted at the outset that this theory is not complete, especially at the "ultimate" level of representation briefly discussed above. In fact, it might be argued that given the state of our current neuroscience and technology, such a theory at that level simply cannot be complete, although educated guesses consistent with the evidence at more behavioral levels can be made. However, even without hubristic and primitive attempts to solve the ultimate problem of representation at the brain level, it is possible to construct and test a theoretical framework that yields a better understanding of representation at the level of experience and of reportage. This framework, as will be seen, may finally yield an understanding of why people pet sharks, and lose spacecraft, and house their best weapons in obsolete forts.

5

Gestalt and Feature-Intensive Processing: Toward a Unified Model of Human Information Processing

Let us begin with the level that must remain incomplete at this time and in this volume, the ultimate level of representation: the place, or space, or quantum reality where memories exist, awaiting retrieval, modification, or loss. The fundamental nature of representation within the human nervous system may constitute the most important question of psychology and of neurobiology, if not also of philosophy and possibly of theology. Yet few if any compelling answers to this question have been forthcoming.

This lack of positive information on the subject is unsurprising when viewed against the long historical parade of attempts to address the issue scientifically in one way or another. There were at one time relatively simplistic concepts of specific brain areas that in some vague way might hold memories. Such views were perhaps permissible in the nineteenth century when neurology and neurosurgery were in their infancy, and, in a grim related connection, when the ballistic qualities of weapons were different. As is well known, a great deal of what we know about brain function derives from the consequences of head injuries, great numbers of which have been caused in warfare. However, prior to the end of the nineteenth century, if one were struck in the head by a bullet powerful enough to obliterate elements of brain, as a general rule one died, with no opportunity to exhibit neurological sequelae. Grapeshot, .69 caliber musket balls, the .44 or .45 caliber bullet fired from the Walker or Peacemaker revolver: all were made of soft lead, and most tended to cause such horrendous tissue damage that it would usually be impossible to investigate the effects on memory of the destruction of specific brain structures.

However, with the advent of smaller bullets for military and general use, with the jacketing of these bullets, and with improvements in military and general surgery, head wounds could be more circumscribed, and more people could survive them, even if the weapons involved were more powerful in terms of sheer momentum and muzzle velocity; the bullets might traverse the skull, rather than being more likely to splatter within it. These factors are operative today; anyone who has worked for long in the forensic realm has encountered cases in which modern, relatively small-caliber bullets have traversed victims' brains but left the victims alive, frequently with specific new behavioral damage related to the areas traversed.

More head-trauma victims also survived as the twentieth century progressed, of course, because of better medical techniques and concomitantly better survival rates for those with head injuries, including those caused in the service of an increasingly mechanized, and therefore dangerous, mass industry.

Thus through the first half of the twentieth century, evidence became available that a bullet traversing the skull, or an industrial accident resulting in head trauma, might kill you, paralyze you, or cause anterograde or retrograde amnesia for a given period. However, it never left memories of 1910 and 1912 intact while losing those from 1911. Something was wrong; the anatomical mansions of the brain did not house memories of the mind within specific rooms, at least not in any way analogous to human architecture or to typical human thinking about space. By 1950, the finding of Karl Lashley and others that they could not isolate a spatial nature for the "engram" strongly suggested that the search be taken up in some other place (Rilling, 1996).

So where were the memories? There was the search for some form of "memory molecule" which reached its rather dubious apotheosis in the early days of the "Worm Runner's Digest" and reports of the mnemonic achievements of cannibalistic planaria (e.g., McConnell, 1964). Many psychologists will recall the excitement generated by the idea that a planarian, a flatworm, could learn something admittedly rather simple, and then be ground up and fed to a planarian colleague which would then "know" the information which its erstwhile comrade had been taught (McConnell, 1962). It was also shown that planaria regenerated from the tail segments of trained ancestral planaria at the third generation exhibited some level of savings of the original training (e.g., Rilling, 1996). Taking this work at its face

value, the conclusion that a "memory molecule" existed seemed inescapable (e.g., McConnell, 1964). However, although anecdotal reports of successful replications of the "cannibalism" studies exist, the phenomenon was effectively unreplicable as a general rule. McConnell's own penchant for humor and for failure to take himself (and others) very seriously also did not help his cause, and serious research interest in this area essentially dried up. The idea of chemical memory is of course still active in a weaker form; a variety of neurotransmitters, for example, have of course been implicated over the years in various aspects of memory and memory context (e.g., Shepherd, 1994). However, since memory occurs in the brain, and since the brain is an electrochemical organ dependent for its functioning on its neurotransmitters, it would be odd, if not miraculous, if specific neurotransmitters were *not* involved in memory.

More recently, there was the very promising approach of the "hippocampus as a cognitive map" in the late 1970s and early 1980s (e.g., O'Keefe & Nadel, 1978), under whose general auspices work is still proceeding. Today, however, ideas of ultimate representation in specific anatomical loci or chemical infrastructures have begun to give way to dramatically more abstract concepts; modern ideas of ultimate representation lie in ideas of the hoisting of quantum realities (e.g., King, 1997; Satinover, 2001) or of processes of self-organization (e.g., Vetter, Stadler & Haynes, 1997). There is even the idea that memories might derive in some manner from the binary code which could occur in some neural analogue of J.S. Bell's molecular bifurcation theorem (e.g., Bell, 1987; Penrose, 1989).

The quantum concepts are of course conjectural, not to say speculative in some cases, and there is simply no empirical evidence for any of them, although very ingenious arguments and analogies have been developed to confirm their possibility. One might notice, perhaps somewhat less than charitably, that many of the loftier theories of representation have been produced by mathematicians, philosophers, and physicists, rather than by the psychologists and neurobiologists who actually deal with the realities of mind and brain on a concrete, empirical, everyday basis. Some of the most exciting and exotic modern theories do have a somewhat abstract flavor, and do not seem to be much concerned with brain/behavior relationships in the traditional sense. Be that as it may, however, "memories" to a great degree have largely ceased to be nouns (structures, cells, or molecules) or even verbs (as in the notion of storage in the rever-

beratory activity of hypothetical hippocampal neural circuits) and now seem to reside halfway between the noun and the verb, in the shadowy interstitial netherworld of the quantum spaces that are presumed to define reality in such complex systems as the brain.

Again, hard empirical evidence of such quantum representations has not been forthcoming, nor is it likely to turn up in the near future. The necessary technology to address quantum representations or submolecular emergent processes simply does not exist. Even if these accountings are accurate, we may never know.

So, if we are technologically unable to provide a coherent account of the ultimate nature of information processing and representation in the brain, we are forced to fall back on functional analysis, to describe not so much what information *is*, but how it *behaves*. In the absence of the technology needed to address the physical basis of the engram at the ultimate level, this type of functional analysis is likely to remain the most comprehensive explanation of human memory for the foreseeable future.

How can this functional analysis best be accomplished? The behavior of information under various task conditions, as shown in the studies discussed thus far, can provide perhaps the best clues that exist to the nature of representation and processing at the functional level, the level that is the focus of virtually all psychological enquiry at this time in the history of the science.

Up to this point in the present volume, the primary types of information addressed in this manner have been the verbal and the imageric. Verbal information, as discussed above, is predominantly semantic or relational in nature. Imageric or pictorial information typically involves more item-specific visual detail. Could this be the linkage between verbal and pictorial information? Is the common ground between the verbal and pictorial realms the level of item-specific or relational information inherent in given stimulus items?

Let us approach this question by reviewing, in light of the arguments developed to this point, precisely what is meant by a visual "image," an internal representation of an external picture. As mentioned above, the concept of the image was familiar to Aristotle, and of course to the Greek and Roman mnemonists, who routinely used imagery in their construction of artificial memory aids (Yates, 1966). The idea of the image has cropped up periodically in epistemological and psychological study ever since. Wilhelm Wundt (e.g., 1897) and a number of other early experimental psychologists saw imag-

ery as a crucial element of psychology and of mental life, so it is somewhat surprising that the concept of the image as a serious psychological construct was assassinated almost at the inception of the modern experimental age. Watson's (1913, 1924) rejection of the validity of internal mental life as the subject of serious study set the pattern for the next six decades, resulting in the concept of the purely "propositional" nature of the image (e.g., Pylyshyn, 1973) so familiar to the artificial intelligence community of the 1970s and 1980s.

However, again as mentioned above, chinks in the armor of this admittedly parsimonious concept began to show within a decade of its widespread inception. Paivio's development and empirical support of the dual-coding hypothesis (e.g., Paivio, 1966, 1971, 1990; Paivio & Csapo, 1969, 1973; Paivio & Yuille, 1969) might be considered the first major salvo, followed in relatively short order by the results of Kosslyn's scanning paradigm (e.g., Kosslyn, 1980; Kosslyn, Ball & Reiser, 1978), the seminal mental image rotation work of Shepard and colleagues (e.g., Shepard & Metzler, 1971), and a host of other studies that demonstrated fairly conclusively that imageric information is processed very differently than is verbal material, and that therefore images must be concluded to possess a separate reality from their verbal counterparts. Images act like pictures, and words don't. It is probably safe to say that by the time of Kosslyn's seminal work (1980), and certainly by the early 1990s, most cognitive psychologists, if not all cognitive scientists, were convinced that images exist and that, whatever they are, they certainly aren't words or amalgams of verbal propositions. Moreover, the pictorial nature of images had become clear, especially in the ingenious work of Shepard, Kosslyn, and Paivio, as discussed above. At a functional level, then, one could by the mid-1980s say fairly conclusively that an image is an internal analogue of a given segment of external visual reality.

Now, if this were in fact the case, there would have been very little room for the kinds of issues developed in the previous chapters, in which we have been searching and gathering evidence for unifying continuum linkages between visual images, auditory images, and verbal representations. If an image is really an internal picture of some sort, then the concept of shared processing resources with the verbal realm, the notion of continuum with auditory imagery and with verbal material, and the idea of representational malleability in the face of different task demands are effectively mean-

ingless. Yet the existence of such shared processing resources, such functional continua, and such representational demand dependency at the experiential level have, as discussed in detail in the preceding chapters, been empirically demonstrated. How can these conflicting ideas be reconciled?

By the 1980s, the imagery camp had effectively scored a decisive victory over the propositional team (Sharps, 1990; Sharps & Nunes, 2002). Victories are seldom scrutinized carefully for signs of inadequacy. And yet, again as mentioned above, there were some problems with the idea that an image is a picture, and even in the idea that it is *like* a picture, which began to surface quietly even as the victory was consolidated.

Let us now consider these problems in some depth. Over the past decade and a half, the mental rotation literature has proved particularly telling in this regard. For one instance, when a person mentally rotates two stimulus elements of different sizes in a standard MR paradigm, those elements rotate at the same rate as elements of the same size (Jolicouer, Regehr, Smith & Smith, 1985). This, at least intuitively, should not be the case. To compare two pictures of different size, one should have to "zoom" (Kosslyn, 1980) them to equivalent size for comparison, a function that should require real time. And yet it doesn't.

Consider also the problem of complexity effects (Cooper & Podgorny, 1976; Folk & Luce, 1987; Sharps, 1990). In physical, real-world pictures, complexity makes no difference to the speed of their rotation. One can of course physically rotate any painting of any degree of complexity, the canvas in its frame, with the same celerity as any other. The complexity, the level of item-specific detail crowding the canvas per se, is utterly irrelevant to the speed with which the entire painting can be manipulated; if an image is directly analogous to a physical real-world picture, then complexity should make no difference to rotational speed at all.

Now, this is sometimes true of *mental* rotation of images as well as of the physical rotation of actual pictures; the two-dimensional rotation of alphanumeric stimuli and of simple Attneave-Arnoult figures (Attneave & Arnoult, 1956) tends to result in the same speed of rotation for complex and simple figures (e.g., Cooper, 1975). However, the rotation of three-dimensional Shepard-Metzler figures typically results in slower processing for complex than for simple figures. In one study (Sharps, 1990), two-dimensional figures designed

to look as much as possible like flat analogues of 3-D Shepard-Metzler elements yielded significant complexity effects as well. Therefore, the complexity-effect distinction between different types of stimuli cannot be a direct function of their dimensionality. Several different aspects of different types of mental images influence the presence or absence of complexity effects in mental rotation frameworks, in a manner wholly unlike anything that would be expected in the world of external pictorial reality. Something else, something decidedly unpictorial, must be going on in the processing of mental images.

This is not, of course, to return to the propositional concepts that governed the concept of imagery prior to the image-as-picture revolution of the 1980s. Quite the contrary. It is obvious, after a quarter of a century of hard empirical experimentation and verification (e.g., Kosslyn, 1980; Paivio, 1975, 1990) that images have a functional reality that cannot be fully explained in terms of the manipulation of propositional codes, even if some form of propositional code represents the most fundamental level at which mental images exist. This is not a yes/no situation, with images existing either as pictures or as series of disembodied propositional codes. Images are something else.

But what? Clearly, mental images are typically processed differently from verbal materials. And yet disturbing results, such as the "zoom" and complexity findings described above, continue to surface fairly regularly. Imageric materials are clearly different from verbal materials; and yet they are not pictures. How can this be reconciled?

There is an interesting tendency, generally shared among experimental psychologists, to deal with mental events such as thoughts, memories, images and verbal traces, as if they were real "things," with nameable, reifiable identities. It is certainly convenient to do this, and perhaps very necessary: it is difficult to see how one would study something as nebulous and ethereal as a memory or a thought without naming it. Nevertheless, one might wonder whether this reification of concepts for convenience may not have leaked over, so to speak, into our conceptions of the basic nature of psychological reality itself. Paivio's initial, elegant work (e.g., Paivio, 1966, 1971; Paivio & Csapo, 1969, 1973; Paivio & Yuille, 1969) dealt in no uncertain terms with "images" and "words," as has virtually every study in this area since that time. This type of early, necessary

reification may have become ossified in a way that may not be entirely productive, descending through the history of the field in even
the most sophisticated theories. Hunt and Einstein's enormously
valuable theoretical distinction between item-specific and relational
information (e.g., Hunt & Einstein, 1981) yields a concept of information that is often very much construed in this manner: item-specific and relational information seem to be nouns, real *things*, with
real, discrete, physical boundaries of some type. A given piece of
information may of course be dealt with in terms of item-specific
characteristics (shapes, visual details, etc.), or in terms of relational
information, such as the category membership of the given item.
But in much of the literature, there seems to be no doubt that the
item-specific and relational characteristics of a given item are those
of an *item*, something real with a reifiable identity.

This is also true of Tulving's (1982) complex theory of synergistic ecphory. In Tulving's basic concept, peripheral and central traces
in memory synergize to result in different levels of memory performance. Of course, the characteristics of peripheral and central traces
differ, and this might seem to provide evidence that these traces have
a reality as discrete and empirically separable stores, as *kinds of things*
in their own right.

Perhaps the most powerful and influential theory along these lines
has been the elegant work of Baddeley (e.g, 1976, 1986, 2001;
Baddeley & Hitch, 1974, 1993; Baddeley & Logie, 1992). As we
have seen, his working memory theory clearly carves the characteristics of any given memory, at least for the short term, into two isolable
and reifiable entities; imageric materials are processed by means of
a visuospatial "sketchpad," whereas verbal entries find their way
into a phonological loop; these two systems are yoked to a central
executive, an entity which is logically required to provide needed
integration and resource allocation. Thus the existence, at least at a
functional level, of distinguishable mental pictures and mental words
is effectively taken for granted.

How well does this separation of powers within the mind, so to
speak, actually capture empirical reality? As a framework for the
study of mental phenomena, this type of reified classification is of
course very useful, but as a veridical picture of the actual nature of
the mind, this type of hypothetical structural segregation of mental
processes is probably not particularly accurate, for all of the reasons
discussed in the preceding chapters. We must have labels of conve-

nience, of course, and being able to refer to images or to words, to working memory or to long-term storage, is essential; one cannot very well progress in the science if one has no terminology with which to refer to the subjects under study. Yet this application of labels of convenience, with their implicit carving-up of cognitive processing, is a two-edged sword. Things in the external world have, as we have seen, discrete boundaries and particular properties, and these are relatively long-lived when compared with the duration of the things themselves. In other words, the major defining properties of things tend to survive as long as the things do. A cement mixer remains a cement mixer, with the qualities of a large portable machine which makes cement. It does not fade in and out of being a forklift or a badger, nor does it occasionally take some time off to whip up a little popcorn. Yet in a very real sense, this type of changeling behavior is precisely what we have seen in the visual, auditory, and verbal cognitive realms across the adult life span. A slight adjustment of the demand characteristics of a given cognitive task can result in parity or huge disparity between the memory and processing performance of young and older adults exposed to the same or to entirely different stimulus types. Although pictures remain pictures and words remain words in the external world, how the internal representations of those items are configured and processed has also been shown to be a very strong function of task demand. Auditory images sometimes behave as if they were words, and sometimes as if they were pictures.

Ultimately, we may state, with considerable empirical backing, that the defining qualities and properties of mental entities, of representations and processes, do not endure as long as do the entities themselves. The things of the mind, so to speak, the representations of words, pictures, and auditory images that somehow inhabit the interstitial quantum spaces of the brain, actually *do* behave like a cement mixer that can cook popcorn or act like a forklift; memories, images, representations, and allied cognitive processes are malleable and mutable in a way that the concrete objects typical of everyday experience in the external world are not. Cognitive "things" are capable of changing in the face of novel psychological exigencies, effectively on demand.

This is really the crux of the argument: *on demand*. Things in external reality do not in general blend their boundaries, their functional characteristics, or their resource bases with reference to task

demand. Visual mental images, auditory mental images, and internal verbal traces appear to do so regularly and predictably, with systematic reference to the types of task demands faced by the minds in which they are resident.

And yet, even in the face of all this mutability and malleability, there appear to be limits surrounding the degree to which representations can depart from their original types. Although pictorial images do not behave precisely as pictures, they clearly have a more imageric character than do words. Any other perspective would effectively return us to the propositional realm of the early 1980's, negating all of the important evidence derived from empirical work on imagery (e.g., Shepard & Metzler, 1971; Kosslyn, 1980; Paivio, 1990) conducted over the past thirty years.

So, if imageric items in the mind are neither mental pictures nor mental words, but are instead nebulous entities which can take on different functional characteristics in response to exigency, then what kind of entities are they? Why are they distinguishable from verbal representations at all? What results in the evident appearance of two "kinds" of information in the brain, one verbal and one imageric, which are processed in functionally interdependent but nevertheless separate systems (Paivio, 1990)? In view of all of these considerations, it becomes possible to see why we have had so much difficulty in isolating and understanding these systems over three decades of solid empirical effort. But what are the connecting, unifying principles that make it possible to reconcile these considerations?

Recapitulation of Evidence thus Far

Let us reconsider, briefly, the most important considerations from the preceding chapters that bear directly on these questions. Consider research on cognitive aging which addressed the evident distinction between imageric and relational processing. Older adults are known to experience relative difficulty in the processing of imageric information (Dror & Kosslyn, 1994; Sharps & Gollin, 1987; Sharps, 1990, 1997; but see also Hertzog et al., 1993). Thus task situations which place greater demands on imageric processing (e.g., Paivio, 1990) are subject to greater age-related change, whereas tasks which deal with relatively preserved verbal, semantic or relational processing (e.g., Nebes, 1990; Wingfield, Lindfield & Kahana, 1998) are much less influenced by age. Within any given memory task, the elderly are probably better at using verbal, relational materials than

they are at dealing with imageric information, although under specific task conditions the elderly can use imageric support for recall at a high level (e.g., Craik, 1986; Sharps & Gollin, 1987, 1988; Sharps, 1991; Sharps & Price-Sharps, 1996; Sharps & Antonelli, 1997; Sharps & Martin, 1998; Sharps & Price-Sharps, 1996). So, demand characteristics influence performance strongly across the adult life span.

What unifying principle underlies this task-dependency of imageric and verbal performance? As discussed above in detail, cognitive asynchrony theory (Sharps, 1997; Sharps & Antonelli, 1997; Sharps & Gollin, 1987b, 1988; Sharps, 1998; Sharps & Martin, 1998; Sharps, Foster, Martin & Nunes, 1999; Sharps, Martin, Nunes & Merrill, 1999) provides an explanation within the asynchronous effects of the generalized cognitive slowing which is inherent in the aging process (e.g., Birren, Riegel & Morrison, 1962; Cerella, 1990). Consistent evidence supporting this formulation has derived from mental rotation studies, spatial memory studies, and studies of recall using the category superiority effect (CSE) as model systems. It has been repeatedly shown that, in general, significant CSE's are obtained only for verbal materials (Sharps & Gollin, 1986; Gollin & Sharps, 1988; Sharps & Tindall, 1992); the category superiority effect generally vanishes for pictorial materials in young adults. Pictures provide sufficient detail to render category information redundant for young adults (Sharps & Tindall, 1992). This would appear, at first sight, to be evidence for a relatively immutable boundary between the verbal and the imageric internal realms. However, older adults, probably as a result of age-related diminution in the ability to create synchronous representations of complex pictorial stimuli (Sharps, 1997, 1998), yield CSEs for both pictorial and verbal situations. In other words, older people import relational, semantic information into memory tasks in order to support imageric recall. Young adults don't typically need to do so, unless their imageric representations are degraded to a level similar to that of their elders. But when pictures are degraded for young adults through diminished exposure time, the performance of young adults may precisely duplicate that obtained from older adults when they are exposed to standard, nondegraded conditions (Sharps, Wilson-Leff & Price, 1995; Sharps, 1997, 1998). When pictures are degraded by external conditions, the young import relational information to deal with them as images; and when images are degraded internally through the cogni-

tive asynchrony inherent in the aging process (Sharps, 1997), older adults import relational information in the same manner.

So, semantic, verbal, relational information can be imported into a task in direct support of imageric memory. Clearly, there is a functional distinction between the processing of verbally accessible, relatively describable stimuli, and the processing of less verbally accessible items which must be processed in terms of their visual elements and visuospatial relationships.

Now, is it the case that there are two separate systems at work here, so that the visual representational system "calls" in some manner to the verbal one when it needs help? Again, the evidence would suggest not. Although of course different brain structures are activated in the initial processing of verbal and pictorial stimuli, ultimately the representations must come down to the electrochemical communication of the brain itself. How parsimonious is it to suggest that two completely different types of representation are to be found within the behavioral exploitation of this single type of energy? Would it not be more logical, in view of the evidence, to suggest that the imageric or verbal nature of a given representation might have something to do with the demand characteristics of the task involving that representation, beyond the initial verbal or pictorial nature of the originating percept? Certainly this hypothesis would appear to be strongly supported by the intermediary status of nonverbal nonmusical auditory imagery, which was shown in a number of experiments (Sharps & Price, 1992; Sharps, Price & Bence, 1996; Sharps & Pollitt, 1998) to possess the characteristics of verbal or of visual information, or of both, depending entirely upon the task demand characteristics to which respondents were subjected.

The Functional Nature of Representation: Gestalt and Feature-Intensive Processing

So, do we know, at this point, what an image is? At the ultimate level of engrammatic representation, the answer must be no. Again, at that ultimate level of brain dynamics, we lack the technology to find the answer to this question. Do we, however, know what an image is at a *functional* level, with reference to other types of material? Here we have perhaps been more successful. An evaluation of the evidence indicates that we are beginning to understand the nature of an image, and of its relationship to corresponding verbal representations, in part through an understanding of what an image

is *not*. A mental image is not a thing, a reified, discrete entity with relatively concrete and immutable boundaries. Rather, images are at least somewhat malleable in the face of psychological and environmental demands. An image can, to some degree, become a verbal item, and verbal materials can create imageric traces.

But what unifying principles underlie this functional task dependency? Why are words and pictures actually different in the mind at all?

It is suggested that the answer lies in a modification of the Hunt and Einstein distinction (e.g., 1981; Einstein & Hunt, 1980) between relational and item-specific information. It is further suggested that the distinction between the verbal and the pictorial lies in the response of the given stimulus type to task demand characteristics. A good analogy lies in the Swiss army knife; if the blade is extended, a Swiss army knife is a knife. If the can-opener is extended, it becomes a can opener, and so forth. What a Swiss army knife *is*, in terms of *its immediate functional capability at any given moment*, depends upon which of its attributes are deployed to face specific demand characteristics. This is what is suggested here for representation and processing: that the same ultimate representations can be made to behave predominantly either as pictorial or verbal materials, depending upon demand characteristics.

But what, in turn, creates this task-dependency, if not the simple pictorial or verbal character of a given representation? It is the level of *verbally accessible detail presented by a given stimulus situation*, rather than the specific qualities of verbal or pictorial representations per se. Some representations are rich in verbally accessible features; for example, a picture of a horse contains a mane of a particular color, hooves, a coat of particular color and length, etc. Such a picture might be processed more as a feature-intensive, verbally accessible representation than might a more abstract representation such as an Attneave-Arnoult figure (e.g., Attneave and Arnoult, 1956), made up of abstract spikes and blobs that are difficult to describe or name.

The horse would therefore be more amenable to verbal processing of its imageric details; the abstract figure would not. The horse, then, would be more amenable to *feature-intensive processing*, in which its various features and their interrelationships could be named and considered, separately and together. This type of processing, of course, must prove relatively slow. However, it does provide for the

most comprehensive analysis of the configuration, and it also provides for the dual coding, both verbal and pictorial, of the various features of the configuration, strengthening traces for later consideration and thereby probably contributing to more successful reasoning processes surrounding that configuration.

The more abstract figure, the one with fewer verbally identifiable features, would have to be processed in a more holistic or *gestalt* manner, as a relatively unitary figure, based upon its overall configuration. It should be noted here that the term "gestalt" in "gestalt and feature-intensive processing" is related to, and derived from, the work of the early Gestaltists, as will be discussed in more detail in chapter 6. However, the term as used here has a specific and relatively limited meaning by comparison with the rich body of Gestalt theory. Whereas, for the Gestaltists, successful higher-order Gestalt processing involved the full consideration of features and their emergent configurations in context (e.g., Wertheimer, 1945/1982; see also Sharps & Wertheimer, 2000), the present use of the word "gestalt" is much closer to the functional consequences of the basic Gestalt laws of perception (see Koffka, 1935; Köhler, 1947; also see Sharps, 1993, for basic review of the major Gestalt laws), in which features come to be perceived as elements of a whole, and it is the whole which is processed without much further reference to the features which compose it. A good example lies in the "law of common fate," which can readily be illustrated by considering the flight of a v-shaped flock of geese: the mind does not track the flight of each individual goose in the flock, but rather sees the flock *as* a flock, a unitary configuration moving in the same direction and toward the same point in space. This is the source of the word "gestalt" as used here: gestalt processing, in the present sense, is *the relatively holistic processing of a given representational configuration, with limited reference to the specific or defining features of that configuration.*

It is important to realize that both verbal and imageric/pictorial events may possess feature-intensive and/or gestalt qualities. It is *not* suggested that verbal materials are intrinsically feature-intensive, or that pictures are intrinsically gestalt. Complex pictures with relatively identifiable features, such as the horse discussed above, tend toward feature-intensive processing. Simple pictures, or pictures with relatively inaccessible features such as Attneave-Arnoult figures, tend toward the gestalt. A single word, especially one not particularly evocative of imagery, may be processed in a highly ge-

stalt manner; a paragraph of dense complex text would of course prove more feature-intensive if read and successfully understood. Gestalt and feature-intensive processing do not reflect a true dichotomy in any sense. Instead, the processing of any given real-world stimulus item, representation, or event lies on a continuum between gestalt and feature-intensive processing.

This continuum has critically important consequences for the likelihood of success in any domain-specific, task-dependent processing situation. These consequences are outlined in the accompanying figure. Feature-intensive processing provides for comprehensive analysis, appropriate to complex stimuli, and to complex memory, reasoning, and decision-making situations; however, it is likely to prove relatively slow. Gestalt processing is much faster; however, in complex situations, many important details will of course not be considered by means of gestalt processes as discussed here.

The two "types" of processing, the two ends of this continuum, are of course functionally related. For example, feature-intensive processing may, in some tasks and with repeated practice, give rise to gestalt processing. This is especially true of relatively automatic cognitive processes, such as those involved in driving a car, as discussed below. However, there are different domains in which each

Figure 5.1
General Flowchart of Gestalt/Feature-Intensive Processing

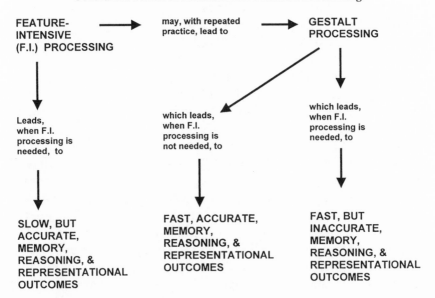

type of processing, each end of the continuum, possesses advantages and disadvantages. For relatively simple or automatized processing situations, with few features that must be considered individually, gestalt processing is clearly superior, especially in situations requiring speed. However, as will be discussed fully in chapter 6, such relatively holistic processing may prove catastrophic in more complex situations, in which specific details must be considered. Under such circumstances, feature-intensive processing will prove superior, although the cognitive processes involved will be significantly slowed.

There is important work in a related tradition that supports these ideas. Chechile, Anderson, Krafczek, and Coley (1996) provided respondents with visual patterns that varied in the complexity of the required interaction of those features. This *syntactic complexity* was shown to have a powerful influence on the speed of item recognition. More complex items, containing the same numbers of visual features, required more time for successful retrieval. The processing of the relationships among internal elements of the patterns altered the nature of the processing.

Chechile et al. interpreted this as evidence for syntactic pattern recognition, in which the representation of visual patterns is made up of sets of propositions. Chechile's visual figures exhibited a pattern of processing similar to that suggested by the present considerations; pictorial items were shown to have a syntactic/semantic logic to them which emerged under the proper task demands. This propositional logic effectively constituted the mechanism by which the task demands exerted their influence. In other words, and as suggested here, it was the levels of syntactically identifiable features which made the differences in performance.

Consider these findings in light of the work of Hunt and Einstein (e.g., 1981), who, as noted above, proposed the distinction between "item-specific" and "relational" information. Item-specific information includes pictorial details such as the colors and shapes of specific features. Relational information includes relationships among the elements of a given stimulus array, and also includes most forms of verbal or propositional data. The syntactic complexity manipulated by Chechile et al. constituted, in effect, a form of relational information, clearly adding relational complexity as syntactic relationships multiplied. Such relationships are themselves features which can be expressed verbally (in the sense of "one more," or "to the right," or "including the following"). A visual configuration rich in

such relationships, then, would be relatively easy to process in verbal terms, and relatively "feature-intensive" as a result; the verbally expressible relational features would allow greater precision to specify the elements of an image, but would require more time to process. On the other hand, a configuration possessing few such relational features would have to be processed in its imageric entirety, as a gestalt.

Clearly there would be no absolute dividing line between the verbal and the pictorial. Rather, there would be a continuum between that which is exceptionally verbally accessible/feature-intensive and that which is exceptionally holistic/gestalt. This continuum appears to be similar to the continuum between the verbal and the visually imageric, with auditory imagery somewhere in the middle, as demonstrated in the work discussed in the preceding chapters.

The gestalt/feature-intensive (G/FI) representational concept, if correct, would help to explain many of the mysteries still to be resolved in the cognitive literature. Paivio (e.g., 1966, 1971, 1986, 1990; Paivio & Yuille, 1969) found that more concrete nouns lend themselves more to imagery than do more abstract nouns; this makes far more sense if there is a continuum uniting the pictorial with the verbal than if these two information types exist as reified entities, separated by an immutable discrete distinction.

Moreover, consider what happens when one conjures up an image of a concrete item with complex features. If one thinks of a zebra, for example, one can see stripes in the image but cannot, in general, count them. If one thinks of an office building, the resultant image is not typically of a precision that would allow an accurate count of the windows. Such precise details are not typically extant in an imageric representation, although they certainly are extant in actual pictures and, of course, in other areas of visual reality. But if one allows for the concept of a relatively vague, largely verbally mediated feature of "stripes" or of "windows," rather than attempting to account for what happens to those actual, pictorial stripes and windows in the transformation from external reality to internal image, it becomes possible to understand why one can't actually count them in a mental image. The gist of "stripes" or "windows," rather than a veridical pictorial representation of the stripes or windows of the initial external percept, is what is manifested at the experiential level. Therefore, the level of detail necessary to count features is simply not available.

It also becomes possible, at this point, to make sense out of one of the mysteries with which this volume began, the problem of eyewitness identification. It has been shown that the mere verbal suggestion that a structure, such as a barn, was present in a given scene can be sufficient to generate a false imageric memory of such a barn (e.g., Loftus, 1975). The verbal suggestion of a previously unseen element in an observed scene is often sufficient to stimulate the observer to recall having seen that element, even if no such element was present in the initial percept.

This is very difficult to understand in terms of an absolute distinction between the picture and the word, except in terms of relatively vague statements about the unspecified influence of beliefs and persuasion upon memory. However, this type of memory reconfiguration becomes relatively easy to explain if the verbally expressed item can functionally and to some degree *become* the pictorial or imageric element. A witness sees a gun being used in the commission of a crime. The witness does not know enough about guns to create mentally isolated summaries of the details of the particular weapon initially observed (calibre, metal finish, type of action, etc.) So, the weapon is encoded without much in the way of feature-intensive processing; it enters the cognitive system as a rather vague, amorphous, nebulous, gestalt/holistic image of "gun." When another gun is seen, if it is sufficiently similar in its overall gestalt qualities to the weapon observed in the initial percept, effectively passing some level of threshold recognition, the new weapon becomes, in the mind of the witness, the one initially employed. A more sophisticated witness might, of course, make a better identification through more feature-intensive processing: "No, this weapon has a bull barrel, and the first one was a target model; no, this one has a shrouded hammer; no, that one was a double-action, and this one is a single." But few people in the modern world know one set of gun features from another, and ultimately, this potentially crucial type of eyewitness evidence may boil down to a vague, gestalt, "gun." If that initial gestalt were no more than "weapon" or "threatening object," one could also understand the relatively infrequent but still occasional instances in forensic practice when a gun metamorphoses into a knife, or when a baseball bat becomes a two-by-four. The crucial distinction here is not picture versus word, or verbal set of features versus pictorial set of features. It is the degree to which processing is either "feature-intensive" or "gestalt," as defined here,

based upon the availability of actual veridical features in the representation at the experiential level.

To summarize, we know that there is an empirically demonstrated distinction between imageric and verbal processing. However, there is also abundant evidence of transformative qualities linking these two "types" of processing in a functional continuum, rather than maintaining them as discrete entities processed in separate functional systems. Therefore, it is suggested that this functional "distinction" might be better explained in terms of unified representations which exhibit either verbally accessible, feature-intensive processing characteristics under appropriate stimulus and demand characteristics, or more gestalt, holistic, non-verbally accessible characteristics under other demand and stimulus characteristics. Such a continuum between the verbal and the imageric representational realms avoids or explains many of the problems, discussed above, which are inherent and unavoidable in a discrete model of two rigidly segregated processes operating in relative isolation.

An Experimental Test of this Hypothesis

It was possible to provide a direct test of this suggestion. If these considerations are correct, the distinction between relatively verbally accessible, feature-intensive processing and relatively non-verbally accessible "gestalt" processing should be demonstrable *within the pictorial modality alone*, using stimulus items which either possess relatively verbally accessible details, or which possess details which are not verbally accessible and must therefore be processed in a more "gestalt" manner. In other words, it should be possible to create an analogue of the verbal/pictorial distinction within the pictorial realm alone, discarding the verbal realm for the moment, and basing this analogue on the relative availability of verbally accessible features. Such a demonstration should result in data consistent with three specific hypotheses:

1.   Pictorial items of the same size and number of elements should require more time to process if their configuration makes it readily possible to identify verbally accessible features, and less time if such features are absent, resulting in the need to process the picture "holistically," in terms of an overall gestalt manipulation.

2.   Pictorial items with more details should be more verbally accessible than less detailed items. Respondents' descriptions of their processing of pictures of the same size and number of elements should be verbally

richer, and therefore require more time, in the cases of items whose configuration makes it readily possible to identify verbally accessible features.

3.   In all of the earlier work from the author's laboratory, cited above (e.g., Sharps, 1997, 1998; Sharps & Antonelli, 1997; Sharps & Tindall, 1992), it has been found that respondents are able to import relational information into tasks to support their recall of pictorial stimuli. Therefore, it would be expected that the repeated processing of feature-intensive items, which are suggested here to share processing characteristics with relational and verbal information, should result in learning which would extend to both feature-intensive and gestalt processing. The reverse, however, would not be expected. There is no evidence that "gestalt" processing should provide a framework for feature-intensive processing. So, any practice effects of gestalt processing should tend to be confined to the same type of processing.

These hypotheses were addressed in separate experiments (Sharps & Nunes, 2002). In the first study, twenty college students were exposed to a mental rotation task in which the two-dimensional items were constructed of the same number of uniform squares, arranged in different patterns. Twenty items were used beyond the normal practice items used in MR studies (see Sharps & Nunes, 2002, for full methodological treatment), and were presented at increasingly large angles between item configurations, yielding a total of 160 item trials per respondent. The patterns were arranged so that the bulk of the squares either lay in the center of the configuration, robbing the subjects of identifiable features which could be verbally described (e.g, "a thing like an L;" "a straight line off to one side;" "a crooked thing at the corner"), or with the bulk of the squares lying more peripherally, in relatively verbally accessible features. The low-feature items were termed, for the sake of convenience, "gestalt" figures; the high-feature items were termed "feature-intensive" figures. It should be noted that these figures differed only in terms of their arrangement into "gestalt" or "feature-intensive" patterns.

The results of this manipulation were entirely consistent with the first hypothesis advanced above. The gestalt figures required significantly less time to process than did their feature-intensive counterparts. Greater angles of rotation of course required significantly more time than did smaller angles, as demonstrated repeatedly in other work (Shepard & Metzler, 1971; see Sharps, 1990, for review of earlier mental rotation literature). The interaction of angle with

item type was also significant. Angle of rotation was more important for response time with feature-intensive than gestalt items. These findings were consistent with the idea that sorting out, monitoring, and retaining internal mental images of specific features would require more time than would be the case for "gestalt" situations in which such manipulations are not possible.

These findings were certainly consistent with the theoretical considerations driving this research. If the semantic, verbally accessible features of nonverbal, pictorial items are in fact processed in the same manner as verbal information, and if this type of processing does not occur with figures which are relatively sparse in such features, then pictorial items *of the same size and number of elements* must nevertheless require more time to process if their configuration makes it readily possible to identify verbally accessible features, and less time if such features are absent. This was precisely what occurred in the first experiment. So, the gestalt/feature intensive (G/FI) distinction suggested above can be identified and produced with reference to the processing dimensions tapped by the MR procedure. There were no explicitly verbal features in the figures used in this experiment, but the addition of nonverbal features that effectively increased syntactic complexity after the manner of Chechile et al. significantly increased processing time. The G/FI hypothesis developed above therefore provides a parsimonious explanation for these results.

Why does the hypothetical distinction between gestalt and feature-intensive processing result in different processing times for the two types of figures? As suggested in the second hypothesis advanced above, feature-intensive figures contain more semantically identifiable elements, and therefore are more verbally accessible, with the consequence that the processing of these items is at least partially verbal/semantic in nature. The results of the first experiment were at least consistent with this supposition. However, there are obviously other competing explanations for these results; how can we know whether or not this explanation is accurate?

If the line of reasoning developed here is correct, we would predict that when respondents are requested to generate verbal protocols describing their processing activities, these would be richer for feature-intensive items than for gestalt items; it should be possible to generate additional verbal activity in support of the rotational processing of more feature-intensive nonverbal stimuli. This was tested in a second experiment, using four feature-intensive shapes and four

gestalt shapes from the first. As before, different rotational angles were used. A new group of thirty college-aged adult respondents was asked to view these figures, to rotate them mentally, and to determine their same/different status in a standard mental rotation task. What was different about this experiment, however, was that respondents were asked to describe their experience and mental activities as they made the rotations. Audio recordings were made of all verbalizations for all of the sessions.

The results of this experiment were entirely consistent with the second hypothesis advanced above. Respondents of course took significantly longer to process larger rotations than shorter ones, and, consistent with the hypothesis advanced, gestalt items produced significantly less verbalization, as measured by time actively spent verbalizing, than did feature-intensive items. Also as anticipated from the results of the first experiment, the interaction of angle with item type was significant, with more verbal description devoted to more feature-intensive items at larger angles of rotation.

So, respondents spent significantly more time in the verbal processing of feature-intensive than of gestalt items. Thus it would appear that feature-intensive items are more amenable to verbal/semantic processing than are gestalt items, as suggested. It should be noted, of course, that both gestalt and feature-intensive items in this study were abstract groupings of squares that lent themselves very little to verbal exposition. Therefore, it would seem that the most parsimonious explanation for this result is that feature-intensive processing of a relatively direct and verbal nature was responsible for the increased verbalization surrounding the feature-intensive items, processing which was suppressed with the less feature-intensive gestalt materials.

The first experiment in this series demonstrated the chronometrically distinguishable characteristics of gestalt and feature-intensive processing. The second showed that feature-intensive items are more amenable to verbal/semantic processing than are gestalt items. What about the third hypothesis, the idea that feature-intensive items might provide practice support for gestalt items, even within the relatively nonverbal realm of the MR paradigm? In earlier work conducted with pictorial and verbal items in both young and older populations (e.g., Sharps, 1991, 1997, 1998; Sharps & Antonelli, 1997; Sharps & Martin, 1998; Sharps & Tindall, 1992) it was shown that both young and older-adult respondents were fully able to "import" relational information into tasks to support their

recall of pictorial stimuli as needed. Therefore, it would be expected that the repeated processing of feature-intensive items, which share processing characteristics with relational and verbal information, should result in learning that would extend to both feature-intensive and gestalt processing.

The reverse, however, would not be expected; there is no empirical reason to suggest that gestalt processing would provide a framework for feature-intensive processing, and so any practice effects of gestalt processing should be confined to the same type of processing. Furthermore, gestalt processing should prove to be less flexible than feature-intensive processing. In feature-intensive processing, discrete features can be considered relative to one another and in different potential combinations, a process that would be expected to facilitate learning which should extend to any related type of processing. Gestalt manipulations as defined here, on the other hand, are necessarily confined to the holistic manipulation of the entire stimulus item, with no internal flexibility from which to learn. Therefore, it would be expected that the repeated processing of feature-intensive items, which are suggested here to share processing characteristics with relational and verbal information, should result in learning which would extend to both feature-intensive and gestalt processing. A reverse effect, with gestalt practice providing for enhanced feature-intensive processing, however, should not occur. There is no basis for supposing that gestalt processing would provide a framework for feature-intensive processing. Again, any practice effects of gestalt processing should therefore be confined to the same type of processing.

These suggestions led to the prediction, advanced above as the third hypothesis in this series, that practice effects, in terms of diminution of response time, should accrue to the processing of gestalt stimuli from the preceding processing of feature-intensive stimuli, but not the other way around. (Moderate practice effects would of course also be expected to occur within homogeneous feature-intensive and gestalt stimulus sets).

A new experiment was conducted to test this question (Sharps & Nunes, 2002). Forty-eight adult respondents were randomly assigned to one of four conditions:

1.   Respondents were shown twenty feature-intensive stimuli followed by twenty gestalt stimuli (the "Feature-Gestalt" condition).

2.   Respondents were shown twenty gestalt stimuli followed by twenty feature-intensive stimuli (the "Gestalt-Feature" condition).

3.   Respondents were shown forty feature-intensive stimuli ("Feature-Feature").

4.   Respondents were shown forty gestalt stimuli ("Gestalt-Gestalt").

The items employed were the ten-square items of the first experiment in this series, and the procedure was the same except for the order of presentation.

To obtain practice effect scores, each group of forty items was divided into quadrants by order of presentation. Mean scores were computed for each quadrant of items, and a quadrant practice effect score computed through the subtraction of each respondent's mean first quadrant score from his or her fourth quadrant score. Not surprisingly,

> the results of this experiment were consistent with the hypothesis advanced. The effect of quadrant was significant; there was a significantly stronger practice effect for the feature-gestalt condition than for either of the homogeneous conditions, the practice effects for which were in turn significantly greater than the effect for the gestalt-feature condition, which in fact was a *negative* practice effect (first quadrant performance was superior to second quadrant performance in that condition). Feature-intensive processing was shown to produce a practice effect for gestalt processing, although the reverse effect was not obtained, exactly as anticipated.

Conclusions Drawn from this Series of Experiments

What can we conclude from the results of these three experiments? The MR task situation chosen for these experiments was a relatively nonverbal, nonsemantic framework, using pictorial stimuli consisting of abstract shapes. Within this framework, "gestalt" shapes required less time to process than did feature-intensive items, and the rotation of feature-intensive items required more time for longer angles of rotation than did their gestalt counterparts.

It was also shown that feature-intensive items were more associated with verbal, semantic processing than were gestalt items, as predicted, in that the processing of the feature-intensive items was associated with significantly greater levels of verbal description than was the processing of the gestalt items. Even with the relatively nonverbal visual abstractions addressed in this series of experiments, feature-intensive items were more amenable to verbal/semantic processing than were gestalt items. In other words, the elements of the

feature-intensive figures behaved more like verbal elements than did the features of gestalt items, a result which is the essence of the theoretical considerations advanced above.

Finally, significant practice effects of feature-intensive processing upon gestalt processing were observed, but not the reverse; the pattern of practice effects predicted by the G/FI theory was exactly as anticipated.

What do these findings suggest? Before we can address this question, we must reiterate what these findings do *not* suggest. Although feature-intensive processing is expected to prove typically more verbally accessible than gestalt processing, this must not be taken to imply that feature-intensive processing is the same thing as verbal processing. The important thing to realize, again, is that both feature-intensive and gestalt processing can occur with both pictorial/visual-spatial processing and with verbal/semantic/relational processing. The cardinal point across processing types is the availability of features that can be used to anchor the cognitive representations involved. Again, and especially in view of the results obtained in the second experiment in this series, feature-intensive processing should prove generally more verbally accessible than more gestalt processing. However, it must be noted that the three MR experiments conducted in this series were designed *in an entirely nonverbal context*, using nonverbal abstract pictorial items as stimulus materials, and that the G/FI continuum of processing was demonstrated within this abstract pictorial stimulus context. The G/FI considerations advanced here therefore appear to apply across stimulus types.

It should also be noted that the figures used in these experiments *did not differ in anything other than their configurational arrangements*. In other words, the same raw amount of visual material was present and processed in both gestalt and feature-intensive figures. The only difference lay in the arrangement of blocks into specific features in the latter case, or into relatively amorphous configurations in the former. Thus the pattern of findings generated appears to have resulted solely from the level of G/FI processing created by the stimulus types and by the demand characteristics of the experiments.

The gestalt/feature-intensive processing continuum appears to provide a parsimonious explanation for the difficulties inherent in the pictorial/verbal processing distinction which is so ubiquitous in the literature. This explanation is consistent with the evidence developed here and with that obtained by other experimenters. Within

this framework, it is not necessary to explain how two completely different kinds of processing, the verbal and the pictorial, can co-exist passively in the chemical soup of the brain with effectively no interaction or melding, to be combined only in specific, directed, voluntary ways when the owner of the brain in question confronts specific task frameworks requiring such interactions. G/FI theory, as advanced here, would replace this logically untenable situation with a continuum of processing based on the availability of identifiable features inherent in the given representation, and available under the given task demands. Depending upon the task type and upon the level of feature-intensive information provided by initial stimulus items, a variety of different continua of processing, such as the verbal item/auditory image/visual image continuum demonstrated and discussed in chapter 4, will result at the experiential level in predictable and testable ways.

So, in summary, there are clear processing distinctions which have been repeatedly observed between verbal and pictorial materials. The work cited here has shown, however, that these distinctions can be explained in terms of task demand characteristics and in terms of the levels of feature-intensive information available in the given item and the given task context. G/FI theory holds that even within pictorial stimulus situations, in which verbal information is not inherent in the stimulus set, more feature-intensive items will yield fundamentally different patterns of processing performance than will less feature-intensive, more gestalt items. Specifically, feature-intensive items will behave more like constellations or clusters of verbal stimuli, and relatively feature-poor "gestalt" items should not. This is exactly what was observed in the three experiments described in this chapter.

It must be reiterated that these results do *not* suggest that there is no inherent difference between a picture and a word. The perceptual nature of an item coming from external reality of course influences the memory of that item. What is suggested, however, is that at the functional, psychological, experiential level, the feature-intensive nature of the stimulus item, whether verbal or pictorial, is critical for processing. There is of course no absolute, functional propositional identity between the picture and the word in mental processing. One would expect a picture of a tree, for example, to be far leafier, greener, and more textured in the mind's eye than the simple abstraction evoked by the word "tree" presented by an experimental apparatus.

But the operating dynamic in this distinction is the level of feature-intensive information provided by the given stimulus item. Leafiness, green-ness, et cetera are features allowing one to identify a given individual tree; the word "tree" possesses no such features inherently, and would therefore be expected to be processed in a more gestalt manner.

This important point might initially seem counterintuitive: aren't verbal items feature-intensive by definition? No, they are not: features may be verbally describable, but a word such as "tree," simply referring to the category of trees without providing any identifiable features, is in fact a "gestalt" type of processing as defined here: the word must be processed holistically, without the breakdown or analysis that feature-intensive processing makes possible. This is a crucial point. A detailed picture is feature-intensive. A blobby pictorial abstraction is not. A descriptive paragraph is feature intensive. A word such as "tree" is not. As discussed above, the G/FI continuum crosses the lines between the verbal and the pictorial, making it possible at last to reconcile the disparate sets of findings discussed above.

After thirty years' concentrated effort, although the functional differences between verbal and pictorial processing still remain in the records of experiment after experiment, it must be admitted that the two pipelines by which the verbal and the imageric might be segregated in the mind have never been adequately identified. It might therefore be suggested that it is at least more parsimonious to view verbal and pictorial memories as deriving from the same basic energetics and processes of the brain. The difficulty with this idea, however, is that theories of processing at the experiential level have not been able to reconcile the ultimate unity of brain with the necessary boundaries and discrete processes of mind.

The theoretical considerations advanced here make it possible to reconcile the two sides of this crucial conflict. In this formulation, the functional differences between the verbal and the visual derive in large part from the level of gestalt or feature-intensive processing to which a given item in memory is put, as a result of the demand characteristics of the given cognitive tasks and of the availability of accessible features for processing presented by the initial external stimuli.

This framework does no violence to the several dichotomous theories briefly considered above (e.g., those of Baddeley, Hunt & Einstein, Paivio, and Tulving). In fact, the present work is largely an

extension of these earlier elegant formulations. The dichotomies in performance demonstrated by all of these theorists are of course real, extant, and experimentally replicable. What the present research indicates, however, is that these apparent dichotomies are not in fact dichotomous at all levels. They are in fact, so to speak, the twin tips of icebergs, reflecting the extremes of largely hidden continua of representations. The "pictorial" or "verbal" processing characteristics of stimuli which lie along these continua depend on the cognitive task demands to which they are being subjected, on the degree to which those demands emphasize the feature-intensive or gestalt nature of the task in question, and upon the level of feature-intensive information inherently available in any given stimulus item itself.

These findings and theoretical considerations admittedly tell us little of the ultimate nature of representation in the brain itself; but they do, at least, make it possible to understand how the same general type of electrochemical activity, whatever its ultimate nature with reference to the coding of experiences, can give rise to completely different types of processing (e.g., pictorial or verbal) at the experiential level. In light of the very strong fit of existing experimental evidence to the predictions generated by G/FI considerations, and also in light of the earlier elegant work of Chechile et al. (1996) on syntactic complexity, the G/FI theory at the very least must be seen to reflect a parsimonious, testable, and potentially unifying framework for a wide variety of findings in cognitive science. Given the consistency of the evidence with the tenets of this perspective, it seems reasonable to suggest that this framework be subjected to further testing in a variety of cognitive domains.

G/FI and the Processes of Reasoning and Decision-Making

For present purposes, the most important domain in which to undertake further testing of the theory is indicated in the third experiment described in this chapter, the MR study concerned with practice effects. Although practice in feature-intensive processing was shown to contribute to greater efficiency in MR processing that had to be carried out on a gestalt basis, the reverse was not the case; practice in gestalt processing did not contribute to better feature-intensive processing. This finding is of particular importance here. Gestalt processing practice not only failed to enhance feature-intensive processing, but actually appeared to interfere with it. There was

a negative practice effect: gestalt processing experience actually contributed to slower feature-intensive processing. Why?

Let us consider the classic work of Sir Frederic Bartlett (1932) on memory for text. Bartlett's (1932) experiments on long-term memory were the first to demonstrate conclusively that reconfiguration of representation occurs, and that it occurs in the directions of personal belief, gist, and brevity. Memories become shorter and less detailed with time. Memories lose details; in other words, features. In the parlance of the G/FI framework, memories gradually become more "gestalt," more holistic and less amenable to detail-intensive processing.

Perhaps the most famous of Bartlett's (1932) experiments made use of the "War of the Ghosts" story, a tribal legend of the Chinook people in the Columbia River area. This legend, when translated and somewhat modified by Bartlett, included unconventional language and concepts. These concepts, while presumably familiar to the peoples who created the legend, were unfamiliar to Bartlett's British subject population. Bartlett made use of this story in part because he believed that the connections between events and motivation for action would be obscured for his respondents by Chinook concepts of social and mythological landscapes, and would therefore result in rationalization on the part of his European subjects, rationalization which would be used in an attempt to conventionalize the story and thereby introduce errors into memory (Bartlett, 1932: 93).

Bartlett's basic thesis was that memory as the product of the excitation of reduplicative memory traces was untenable. Memory, for Bartlett, was a dynamic process whose features and qualities would be based on schemata acquired by acculturation. A "memory" was not a veridical record of the past. It was a reconstruction of an active and dynamically changing set of internal representations, only roughly related to the external realities of the memory's origin.

As is well known, Bartlett's results from the "War of the Ghosts" studies were consistent with this thesis. The written narratives produced by his subjects were considerably shorter than the original legend, and continued to be abbreviated with repeated reproduction. Details such as the unfamiliar names of geographic locations were lost, and unconventional language, by the standards of normal English usage, was conventionalized.

Although attempts to replicate various aspects of Bartlett's work have met with different levels of success, there can be no question

that such reconfiguration exists; it has recently been shown that his repeated reproduction results can be replicated (Ahlberg & Sharps, in press; Bergman & Roediger, 1999). Earlier failures to repeat these results (e.g., Gauld & Stephenson, 1967; Wheeler & Roediger, 1992; Roediger, Wheeler & Rajaram, 1993; Wynn & Logie, 1992) can largely be reconciled with Bartlett's findings through consideration of methodological differences (Bergman & Roediger, 1999).

Bartlett's work showed that as a memory resides in the mind, the details of initial, external stimulus situations, the features on which feature-intensive processing is based, are gradually lost. Details are apparently relatively fragile by comparison with gist. Even the most vivid visual memories ultimately become reconfigured, with loss of detail and retention of bare gist as the product of memory processing (Bartlett, 1932). Over time, our memories of scenes and pictures become more like our memories of corresponding words in terms of loss of detail. To return to an earlier example, we lose the green-ness and the leafiness, and are left with the relatively featureless gestalt abstraction "tree." Sometimes, again as discussed earlier, we are left with the relatively featureless gestalt abstraction "gun," with potentially tragic consequences for wrongful identification in the legal system.

And yet gist or gestalt processing is of enormous importance. There are many situations in which human beings and other animals must ignore much of the feature-intensive information entering their perceptual fields. A classic example is driving; much of the information which one might gain from billboards, passers-by, the car stereo or one's cell-phone would be far better ignored if the intent is to keep the car on the road and out of collisions. New drivers, if they are to survive to become old drivers, must automatize the coordinated action of clutch and gear shift; the teenaged driver who is trying to remember, in a feature-intensive manner, to move the shift in an "H" is a much greater peril to hapless pedestrians than is the experienced driver who moves the shift automatically, paying no real attention to the details thereof. Gestalt driving is simply better than feature-intensive driving, although the initial phases of learning to drive require much more feature-intensive processing. This is true of many activities, from learning to write in cursive through learning to type, to drive, to shoot a rifle, and to swim. Although empirical proof would be required to validate this statement generally, it might at least be suggested that the skills required to perform many if not

most complex motor activities, activities which in turn require memory of how to perform them correctly, begin as awkward, feature-intensive series of linked actions, and finish as smoothly integrated gestalt behaviors.

Thus it may be advantageous, in some situations, to use feature-intensive processing as the practice that will ultimately become the gestalt, automatized, habitual acts that enable us to function well in such activities as driving in the modern world. A close analogue presumably existed in the ancient world in which humanity evolved, in such activities as spearing prey, fashioning stone tools, making nets, and so forth. As Dorner (1996:6) suggested, ancient hunter-gatherers probably did not typically have to think beyond a given subsistence situation to its ramifications or context, at least not as a general rule. One presumably hunted a given animal, gathered a given edible root, or built a given shelter without the necessity of giving much thought for the relationship of that momentary activity to the larger world or to the greater corpus of one's own life. There would probably have been less of an emphasis, at least in non-social situations, on seeing or dealing with any given practical problem as being embedded in the context of other situations or problems than is the case today.

The upshot of this probable characteristic of our long evolutionary history may be that, mentally, we are generally predisposed to focus on the problem or event at hand, without considering features of the event's context which are in fact pertinent, but which arise from other sources. We may tend to treat the problem at hand as an isolated gestalt, a holistic configuration relatively devoid of the need for feature-intensive analysis, even when this is not in fact the case. As a result, we may simply fail to examine the features of the problem space that arise or have their origin elsewhere.

So, there may be something of a predisposition to use feature-intensive processing primarily in the learning process of mastering complex activities, and then to function more on a gestalt than a feature-intensive level as greater mastery gradually makes this possible. Gestalt processing as defined here is more efficient in many everyday activities, in which it is not necessary to analyze all the details on an ongoing basis, or to look beyond the immediate problem space into its context or at factors which arise from that context. This is likely to be true at least in the routine performance of many complex human activities.

The results of the practice-effects experiment described in this chapter are certainly consistent with this perspective. Feature-intensive MR processing led to better gestalt MR processing, just as feature-intensive learning to drive leads to better "gestalt" driving. This result seems to mirror the normal course of real-world learning events, although it must be admitted that this is hypothetical at this time; additional research will be needed to test the generality of this hypothesis.

Nevertheless, it would appear that when possible and on average, we generally function more in a gestalt mode than in a feature-intensive mode. The difficulty with this, of course, is that when one encounters a situation in which details are important or lethally crucial, to ignore them in favor of habitualized gestalt responses may prove correspondingly catastrophic. Major decisions in a complex world are rarely best left to automatized, gestalt processing.

Are G/FI concepts, as constructed here, really directly applicable to the realm of decision making? At this point, using research in cognitive aging, in auditory imagery, and in the specific realm of G/FI processing itself, a case has been made that considerations inherent in cognitive asynchrony and G/FI processing may be responsible for a wide variety of memory and basic processing phenomena in young and older adults. How large is the leap from this body of data into the realm of complex decision-making?

There is no question that an enormous amount of empirical work remains to tie the findings and considerations presented here to other aspects of basic and applied human cognition. However, it is possible to use considerations derived from the G/FI theory to generate specific testable hypotheses in the realm of decision-making. This is the subject of the next chapter. We have already seen how these considerations apply to the question of faulty eyewitness identification. Now we will apply these ideas to the questions of why people pet sharks, and lose spacecraft, and house their best weapons in obsolete forts.

6

Bad Decisions, G/FI Processing, and Contextual Reasoning

Gestalt processing, as discussed in chapter 5, is apparently the premiere type of processing in routine, complex motor activities such as driving, in which too much attention to detail can be disastrous. However, gestalt processing is probably suboptimal, if not catastrophic, in such activities as deciding whether to marry someone or to bomb another country. Under such task conditions, more feature-intensive evaluation is absolutely necessary to prevent divorce or thermonuclear exchange. But what exactly is gestalt processing, as the term is being used here? How does it operate, mediating success or failure, in the realm of reasoning and decision making?

Gestalt Concepts

The idea of a gestalt concept, as used in the present work, is related to and derived from considerations initially developed by the Gestalt psychologists. A central issue for Gestalt psychology was the way in which the perceptual and cognitive universes are organized, in which disparate elements come together to produce coherent configurations, or Gestalts. The unit of analysis for the Gestaltists was not the detail, the feature, or the element of a given configuration. Rather it was the configuration itself, and the way in which that configuration emerged from fundamental organizational processes. The importance of organization in perception and understanding, central to Gestalt theory, was acknowledged very early in the history of experimental psychology. Wilhelm Wundt (1897; Sharps & Wertheimer, 2000) found the concept to be of significant importance, and the idea of organization was expressed formally in the concept of form by von Ehrenfels (1890). The gist of von Ehrenfels' argument was that a whole, such as a square, is more than the sum

of four equal straight lines plus four right angles. There is also the form quality of "squareness," without which the simple geometric components are effectively meaningless. But it was Max Wertheimer who effectively founded and formalized Gestalt theory. One of the earlier and more crucial demonstrations of Gestalt concepts lay in the phi phenomenon, the phenomenon of apparent motion. At certain intervals, the alternate blinking of a pair of lights gives rise to the illusion that a single light is jumping from place to place. Wertheimer (1912a) pointed out that this strongly challenged the idea that "sensations and perceptions correspond point for point with the local sensory stimuli." The existence of the phi phenomenon proved that the normal human nervous system is capable of generating percepts that do not correspond directly to the mosaic of physical stimulation (Sharps & Wertheimer, 2000: 318). In other words, the whole differs from the sum of its parts; the mind reconfigures the outside world, forming representations which depend upon their organization, as well as upon their components.

Gestalt theory proved to be enormously productive in the first half of the twentieth century, resulting in the Gestalt laws of perception (see Sharps, 1993, for review) and in a tremendous body of solid work addressing everything from musical meaning (Wertheimer, 1910) to the perceptions of non-Western peoples (Wertheimer, 1912b), to the work of Köhler in numerous areas including his famous studies of insight in apes (Köhler, 1925), to the work of Koffka (e.g., 1935) on perception, development, and numerous related topics. There were a host of other offshoots. ("Gestalt" psychotherapy was apparently not among them—the name was chosen based on the admiration of its founder, Perls, for the Gestaltists' work, especially that of Wertheimer [Arnheim, 1974; Henle, 1978; Sharps & Wertheimer, 2000]). Most critically for present purposes, the Gestalt perspective led Wertheimer to his seminal work on productive thinking.

Wertheimer (1945/1982) studied human problem solving, ranging from relatively simple problems such as finding the area of a parallelogram to Einstein's work on relativity. He found that in every case of genuinely productive thinking, in which good and creative solutions were generated in any given problem space, it was crucial for the thinker to consider the elements of the problem space appropriately in context. The relationships among the elements, constituting a Gestalt whole reminiscent of Ehrenfels' "squareness," were

at least as important, if not more important, than the elements themselves.

Now, this may seem to point to a problem with the present formulation. Isn't it the thesis of this work that one must attend to the elements, the features, if good decision-making is to proceed? Haven't we suggested that the holistic, "gestalt" treatment of a decision space, without reference to its features, is a major component of decisions to pet sharks, or failures to convert among metric and English units and thereby crash spacecraft? Wertheimer considered it essential to consider elements themselves (features and details) within the context of a given problem space, not simply to ignore them in favor of holistic processing of the entire gestalt configuration.

This is certainly true. As repeatedly shown by Wertheimer (1945/ 1982), the crux of successful processing is to treat both context and details in any given formulation, to the extent that the task makes that possible. As discussed in chapter 5, the use of the term "gestalt" in the present work differs from this concept of ideal contextual reasoning, in that gestalt processing as defined here is the processing of the whole or the configuration with minimal reference to the elements or details from which that configuration emerges. There are times, as in the case of driving a car, when this type of non-feature-intensive processing is in fact optimal. However, there are other times when the lack of feature-intensive processing may prove catastrophic.

Nevertheless, it would appear at first glance that one might rather seamlessly meld Wertheimer's Gestalt concept of productive thinking with the gestalt/feature-intensive ideas discussed here. Perhaps all one has to do, to accomplish productive thinking in Wertheimer's sense, is to ascertain whether or not one is in a task environment which is more amenable to feature-intensive processing or to holistic/configurational/ "gestalt" processing, as defined here, and then act accordingly, engaging in feature-intensive processing as appropriate to the task and to the degree that the stimulus materials or task elements make possible.

To a limited degree, this is probably true. And yet the whole question is a little more subtle. Central to productive thinking and good decision making, for the Gestaltists, was the concept of *radix*. *Radix* (from the Latin for root) is the critical, central core of information in a given problem or decision space. It is, in effect, the necessary information to solve the problem correctly and productively. That information may come from the specific elements of the problem or

decision space in configuration, or from the interaction of that configuration with its context, depending upon the nature and complexity of the given cognitive task situation.

But how is *radix* developed in any given problem or decision space?

Wertheimer (1945/1982:15) relates the story of his visit to a classroom, in which the teacher had been relentlessly drilling the students on how to calculate the area of a parallelogram. Wertheimer felt that the students had not truly grasped the *radix* of this problem, and that the rote learning to which they had been subjected was not conducive to productive thinking about the geometric realities of which the parallelogram provides an example.

But the students certainly demonstrated that they had grasped *something* related to the problem. Much to the pride and joy of their teacher, the students successfully multiplied the base times the height in an endless stream of parallelograms of differing dimensions. Even without "thinking at all" or having "grasped the issue" (Wertheimer, 1945/ 1982:15), the students had clearly understood something along the following lines: if it looks like a parallelogram, drop a perpendicular to yield the height and measure it, then measure the base, then multiply the one by the other. This was emphatically not productive thinking in Wertheimer's sense, but on the other hand, it certainly got the parallelograms measured.

Wertheimer asked for the opportunity to put a problem to the students. He drew a parallelogram resting on one of its slanted uprights, rather than on its base, so that the figure jutted up at an angle. He asked the students to find the area of this new figure, or rather of this old figure at the new angle. Most of the students, of course, were now utterly unable to cope with the situation, drawing a variety of practically random lines through the figure and its surroundings in an attempt to find some configuration that would enable them to find and multiply a base by a height. Only a few managed to turn the paper to the requisite angle and apply the magic formula.

The students were puzzled, the teacher was miffed, and Wertheimer had shown that the students had not in fact grasped the *radix* at all. They had simply learned, by rote, an automatized (Gestalt, in the sense used in the present volume?) formula; they had no real understanding of the principle that a parallelogram is to be treated in the same way no matter its orientation.

On the other hand, one might reframe this famous demonstration without doing violence to Wertheimer's elegant interpretation. Wertheimer was certainly correct: in terms of the intention of the class, which was presumably to provide an increased sophistication in mathematics, the *radix* of the problem had not been grasped. However, in a way, a different *radix* had been very well understood. The students, under the tutelage of their presumably now-fuming instructor, had begun with classically feature-intensive analysis, as defined above. Learning the corners, angles, line segments and shapes that constitute parallelograms, they had then memorized the features of the formula "base x height = area," and had then memorized the application of the formula to the configuration. They had, in fact, grasped *a radix*, the *radix* of an elegant solution to their major problem from their perspective: when confronted with a whole bunch of these things, do the same rote formula on all of them and you will escape the negative attentions of the schoolmaster.

Wertheimer, in a way, had presented these students with an entirely new problem: one in which the *radix* involved a wholly new element, the context in which the parallelogram was placed and against which it must be evaluated. Wertheimer's problem added a step, something along the following lines: if it's shaped like a parallelogram but it's at a weird angle, turn it until you can tell where the base is, and then do the same rote formula. The problem had changed because the *radix* had changed, at least from the students' point of view, and the *radix* had changed because the new problem required understanding of context. The new problem required the students to reason about that context, and they sadly lacked the information needed for such contextual reasoning. The formation of the new radix required information they simply did not have.

Now, one might say that another phenomenon, that of habit and mental set, had reared its head here, and this would certainly be correct. The students had gotten into the habit of "mindlessly" solving parallelogram problems, and *einstellung* or mental set would certainly be expected to form a major factor in the prevention of truly productive thinking about the problem space, just as in the famous water-jar problems studied by Luchins (1942).

However, although there is no question that habit, functional fixedness, and mental set are powerful barriers to creative or even intelligent reasoning, a great many genuinely bad decisions and mental errors are made in the absence of any opportunity to make the

same decisions earlier and thus learn an appropriately wrong-headed mental set. The mental errors described in Chapter 1 above were generally of this type. People swimming in shark-infested waters, for example, have seldom had the opportunity to do so before. The Mars orbiter technicians certainly did not make the conversion error as the result of practice. Nor, as we have seen, could these things have happened out of ignorance: probably everyone on the planet knows that large sharks sometimes eat people, and the NASA experts were certainly not unfamiliar with the existence of the metric system.

It is, of course certainly true that hindsight is typically better than foresight. Horowitz (personal communication, 2001, December) points out quite correctly that one cannot establish a direct equivalency between a Gestalt concept of "mindlessness" and the simple existence of incorrect decisions as evaluated in the aftermath of those decisions. All of the examples discussed in the present work are of course based on ex post facto reconsideration of decisions that led to negative consequences, with elements that would need to be corrected in the future under similar conditions. Being incorrect in this way does not mean that one is "mindless," even when working with relatively simple decision spaces.

This is certainly true; one cannot in any way establish a lawful equivalency between being "mindless" and being incorrect. Yet at the same time, we might suggest that there are probably functional *commonalities* between the processes underlying classical Gestalt examples of "mindlessness" and those underlying incorrect decisions, commonalities which lie in the realm of information transfer. Again, people are aware that sharks are dangerous; NASA engineers and technicians understand mathematics and measurement. Yet something prevented the necessary transfer of information, already present in long-term memory, into the working memory context of problem space and decision context in each of the examples described. Some sort of functional barrier, somehow inherent in the neural processing of the brain itself, and having consequences at the psychological and experiential level, was present in each case to prevent the necessary information transfer. In reviewing decisions with negative or potentially negative consequences, then, we are not really in pursuit of classical Gestalt concepts, or of the nature of "mindlessness" in problem solving and decision making; rather, we are in pursuit of a much more manageable topic, the question of absent or

attenuated information transfer in specific decision spaces in which the given information would have proven critical.

So what actually happens in such cases? What is it that occurs when the *radix* governing a problem or decision space turns out not to contain crucial information, information that is already in fact known to the respondent?

G/FI Processing, Decision Making, and Contextual Reasoning

Decision making is one of the most important of human activities, but also one of the most enigmatic and least understood. Human beings are literally, by definition (*Homo sapiens sapiens*, "the wise, wise man"), intelligent. And yet human thought is often overshadowed by the failure to use relevant, important, and available information when it comes to actual decision making. Human minds have created space flight, but have also made many simple but important errors in its implementation; witness the catastrophe of the Challenger, the series of errors leading to the failure of Apollo XIII, and the now-famous failure to convert English units to the metric units required by the Mars orbiter (Cowen, 1999). Humans possess the mental subtlety to make pesticides, but fail to contain them appropriately, with well-known consequences for the environment and for human health (e.g., Matthiessen, 1987). Humans have often begun wars with great enthusiasm in the assumption that they would be quick and beneficial, even in the face of the evidence that such outcomes would be unlikely, based on experience with similar situations (Dyer, 1985; Keegan, 1998).

In less earth-shattering examples, the present author has on a number of occasions encountered waterless, hatless nature-lovers in shower sandals, scampering off in summer into rattlesnake- and scorpion-infested regions of the Mojave and Sonoran deserts; seen tourists attempting to descend on foot into the Grand Canyon in open-toed high heels; observed climbers beginning the ascent of icebound peaks in Colorado while wearing shorts, tank tops and sneakers; and watched in open-mouthed astonishment as colleagues jogged in nothing but running shoes and shorts in densely mosquito-infested malarial regions along the Mekong. One can find vast numbers of such examples, both in history and in everyday life. Many of the most egregious, not surprisingly, lie in more complex realms, or in realms in which context is crucial, or in which people have to think about the future consequences of actions in a time-series frame-

work (Dorner, 1996). On the other hand, many examples seem to lie in the realm of the almost incredibly obvious.

How is it that human beings can possess high intelligence and yet evince frequent lack of intellectual awareness in decisions? How can people with reasonable minds decide to pet sharks, or decide to place rifled artillery in defensive fortifications that pose no defense at all against rifled artillery? This paradox of intelligence is of obvious importance, but oddly, there has been very little recent research focused on this question. Older rationalistic concepts (e.g., Simon, 1957) have for some time (e.g, Tversky & Kahneman, 1972, 1973, 1974; Kahneman & Tversky, 1972, 1979) been eclipsed by studies of heuristics and biases (Medin & Bazerman, 1999), which now form the crux of modern behavioral decision research (BDR). BDR has been very successful in approximating and modeling real-world contexts (e.g., Bazerman, 1998; Camerer, 1995; Gilovich, 1992), but has generally focused on errors, rather than on successful decision making (Medin & Bazerman, 1999). Also, with few exceptions (e.g., Freedman & Fraser, 1966; Cialdini, 1988), most modern decision research has focused on game theory and economics, leading to questions of generality to other realms (Garnham & Oakhill, 1994; Payne, 1973, 1982). There has been an increasing call for studies at a deeper level (Medin & Bazerman, 1999) to understand factors such as the influence of contextual processes in reasoning (e.g., Gauvain, 1993; Blanchard-Fields, 1986; Park, 1992; Sharps & Wertheimer, 2000; Willis, 1991). It is in this contextual approach that solutions to the paradox of intelligence may lie.

As we have seen, the Gestalt tradition of research focused on this issue. The Gestalt psychologists (e.g., Wertheimer, 1945/1982; Kohler, 1947; also see Sharps & Wertheimer, 2000, for consideration of classical Gestalt considerations) emphasized the importance of context in reasoning. Again, the Gestaltists showed that if the context of a cognitive task is understood, meaningful solutions will be forthcoming; if not, solutions are likely to be "mindless," wrong or too narrow to be useful (Wertheimer, 1945/1982).

(Incidentally, although much of the classical and modern work on these issues has been concerned with problem solving rather than with decision making per se, there is substantial overlap between the two realms [see Greeno, 1978; Reese & Rodeheaver, 1985]. Much research on real-world problem solving [e.g., Willis, 1996; Denney, 1989, 1990; Park, 1992] has shown that problem solving and deci-

sion making grade into one another and share the same types of processes [e.g., Denney, 1989]. Decision making competence, like problem solving competence, must reflect congruence between the knowledge and skills of the given respondent and the demands of the immediate environment [e.g., Willis, 1995; Grisso, 1986; Lawton, 1982]. This point was strongly emphasized by the early Gestaltists: information relevant to the given cognitive task must be immediately available in the task context to be useful, both in the realms of problem solving and decision making.)

Dorner (1996) has provided an elegant analysis of erroneous decision making, examining responses to complex decision situations presented as computer simulations. Among the most crucial factors contributing to unsuccessful decision making in these simulations were the following (Dorner, 1996:18):

1.   Acting without prior analysis of the situation.

2.   Failing to anticipate side effects and long-term repercussions.

3.   Assuming that the absence of immediately obvious negative effects meant that correct measures had been taken.

4.   Letting overinvolvement in "projects" blind decision-makers to emerging needs and changes in the situation.

5.   Being prone to cynical reactions.

Little in the present research framework can be done about cynical reactions, although it might (cynically?) be observed that people might develop fewer such reactions in a world of better and more rational decision making. Dorner's fourth point is also less than amenable to the kinds of considerations developed here, most likely involving mental set (e.g., Luchins, 1942) and cognitive dissonance (Festinger, 1957). However, Dorner's other three points are most interesting in view of the considerations presented here. Prior analysis of a situation involves context, understanding of what will happen before it happens. So does the failure to anticipate side effects and long-term repercussions, and the failure to see what will happen as a result of bad decisions in the future, even though nothing particularly negative happens immediately. In order to prevent such difficulties, and to understand context in relation to problem solving or decision making in a given instance, one would have to begin by

making a feature-intensive analysis of the relationships between immediate problem space or decision space and potentially influential factors deriving from the relevant context.

Another tradition of research, specifically on text comprehension, is highly relevant here, especially to Dorner's first point concerning prior analysis. In a very well-known study, Bransford and Johnson (1973) showed that virtually incomprehensible passages of text can be rendered both comprehensible and memorable by means of a guiding or organizing picture or relevant simple phrase, presented to respondents just prior to passage presentation. This prior contextual information has a powerful influence on understanding, because text comprehension is determined primarily by three factors— whether the information being learned from the text is related to previous ideas (Kieras, 1978), whether these ideas are still available in short term memory (Lesgold, Roth & Curtis, 1979), and whether these ideas have direct, noninferential linkage to the concept to be understood (Haviland & Clark, 1974). These factors, if present, prevent the need for time-consuming reinstatement searches for pertinent information and organizing frameworks in long-term memory (Glenberg, Meyer, & Lindem, 1987; Kintsch, 1979, 1994; Lesgold, Roth & Curtis, 1979).

To reframe these considerations, relevant information in long-term memory may have little bearing on the comprehension necessary for effective understanding, and thus for effective decision making. Information must be *present in the proximate context of the decision,* immediately available in working memory, in order to be effective.

How can this be? In any given decision context, failure to consult one's own long-term memory implies functional barriers between the elements of mind concerned with the decision space and those concerned merely with the retention of potentially relevant information. However, this concept immediately encounters all of the difficulties with the notion of internal mental barriers that we have already seen. At the same time, though, these difficulties might be solved through the same types of processes that we observed in dealing with the "barrier" between pictorial and verbal information. It turned out that there was no barrier; rather, functionally, the characteristics of different types of mental images and verbal representations turned out to lie on functional continua of gestalt and feature-intensive information. In research on cognitive aging, on auditory

imagery, and on the existence of these continua in pictorial process- ing alone, it has been shown that "barriers" between different types of information can be created, strengthened, attenuated, or elimi- nated by means of relatively simple shifts in task demand character- istics. These shifts, in general, have been concerned with the provi- sion or withholding of feature-intensive information in a given task, or with emphasis on more feature-intensive or "Gestalt" processing.

Is it possible that the same types of manipulations also apply to the realm of decision making? Perhaps, in order to make it possible for individuals to evaluate a given decision thoroughly with refer- ence to their own understanding, knowledge, and experience, it is merely necessary, in the tradition of Wertheimer and the Gestaltists, to modify the framework of the task. Perhaps we must simply make it easier for the respondent to connect his or her perception of the overall Gestalt of the decision space to relevant factors in its con- text, factors that are already present in long-term memory but which are not present in the decision space itself. If this line of reasoning is correct, decision understanding should be improved if a feature-in- tensive "bridge" to relevant factors in the context is provided to the respondent. The simplest way to do this would be to provide this information at the time the respondent begins to evaluate the deci- sion space itself, after the manner of Bransford and Johnson (1973).

Let us summarize this line of reasoning for the purpose of form- ing a testable hypothesis. It is suggested that much of the reason why critical information is often left out of decision making con- texts is because that information, *even if present and available in long term memory,* is not immediately present in the context of the decision. However, if such known information is placed in the im- mediate mental context of the decision space, it should strongly in- fluence outcomes by providing a bridge to an analysis of the rel- evant specific features in the decision's external context. We have already seen, in a number of studies by the author and colleagues, that contextual information can be used by respondents across the adult life span to improve cognitive performance in a wide variety of areas, including spatial memory (Sharps & Gollin, 1987a, 1988; Sharps, 1991; Sharps & Martin, 1998; Sharps, Foster, Martin & Nunes, 1999), mental rotation (Sharps, 1990; Sharps & Gollin, 1987b; Sharps & Nunes, 2002), and nonspatial memory (Gollin & Sharps, 1988; Sharps, 1997; Sharps & Antonelli, 1997; Sharps, Martin, Nunes & Merrill, 1999; Sharps & Tindall, 1992; Sharps, Wilson-Leff & Price,

1995) in both the visual and auditory realms (e.g., Sharps, 1998; Sharps, Price & Bence, 1996; Sharps & Pollitt, 1998). It is therefore suggested that the provision of noninferential pertinent information in the immediate context of a given decision might significantly influence the usefulness and correctness of that decision.

This hypothesis was tested in a recent experiment (Sharps & Martin, in press). Respondents were exposed to twelve real-world decision scenarios that had resulted in negative outcomes. Half the respondents received these scenarios alone, and half were provided with relevant information in the immediate context of the decision. The question was the degree to which this information, present in the immediate context of the given decision rather than dormant in respondents' long-term memory, would aid respondents in the recognition of the negative quality of the decisions.

The scenarios employed were taken from a variety of relatively obscure public sources. (The full set of twelve scenarios may of course be obtained, if desired, from the author.) These decisions were of the "executive" or "larger world" type, including such items as whether students who have completed specific prerequisites can be admitted to specific courses, whether major purchases of computer equipment or personnel shifts are advisable in specific educational and corporate settings, or whether national budget priorities could afford to embrace military or civil agendas under specific circumstances. Decisions used were real, drawn from newspaper accounts, accounts of university activities in professional journals, and similar sources. Some minor details were changed (e.g., names and places were deleted) to avoid any possible embarrassment which might derive from this work, and to avoid any possible familiarity with these scenarios on the part of respondents. All of the decisions used in this research had led to negative consequences (economic losses, exposure to avoidable hazard, or the hampering of desirable outcomes).

The contextual information provided, however, had to be created by the experimenters. It was of obvious importance that the respondents *not be taught anything new* by the information, beyond what they already knew and understood as part of their general knowledge, and that they not experience any bias derived from the experimenters' putative viewpoints. The information with which respondents were to be provided had to be present, already, in their own experiential lexicons, so that the provision of that information sim-

ply reframed the decision space, rather than providing a novel element in that space.

A preliminary study was conducted to ascertain, to the degree empirically possible, that the materials used possessed this quality. A group of respondents read the twelve paragraphs to be used, together with the twelve items of contextual information to be provided to the experimental group of the primary study. A Likert scale required them to rate, on a scale of 1 to 7, the degree to which that information was known and understood to them from their own common sense, intelligence, and education "as you are now." A rating of 1 indicated full understanding and knowledge; the mean score obtained was 1.19, indicating strongly that, as intended, the contextual information to be provided was generally seen by a sampling of adults from the relevant population to be part of their common sense, current knowledge and general intellectual qualities. This information did not provide new or novel knowledge, information, or training.

One hundred and sixteen college students, aged eighteen to thirty-five, participated in the primary study, rating the decisions described in the twelve scenarios as either good or bad, positive or negative. Two versions of the scenario set were used; one, the "basic scenario" version, simply stated the situation and the decision to be made. The other, the "contextual information" version, provided the simple relevant contextual information described above at the end of the each scenario. Again, this contextual information was already well-known to the respondents, in some cases to the point of being fatuous: such informata as the fact that a university is concerned with disseminating information as effectively as possible, and the fact that if money is spent on one thing it won't be available for other things, were provided, clearly not contributing in any crucial way to the education of any normal adult college student. This is a critical point: no new information was provided. The contextual information given required no specialized training of any kind, and was already available to the respondents in long term memory. The information provided was not new to the respondents. It was merely made *immediately available in the task context,* rendering reinstatement search of LTM unnecessary, in the manner suggested by Kintsch (e.g., 1979, 1994).

An intelligence test, the Kaufman Brief Intelligence Test (KBIT, Kaufman & Kaufman, 1990) was also administered to all respon-

dents, to evaluate the degree to which general intellectual capabilities influenced the use of contextual information.

The results of this study were entirely as predicted. The effect of contextual information was significant, yielding an effect size value of .24, very large by the standards established by Cohen (1988). Provision of simple contextual information clearly had a strong effect on decision judgment. No significant difference was observed in the performance of female and male respondents.

Interestingly, multiple regression of decision scores against intellectual abilities as measured by the KBIT revealed no significant relationships. This actually serves to support the arguments made here: high intelligence was clearly unnecessary for successful decision evaluation if the respondent was to make use of the simple contextual information provided. This result is also at least somewhat encouraging: the implication is that individuals without extraordinary intellectual gifts are fully capable of the type of reframing required to understand the negativity of a given bad decision, at least within the framework examined. In other words, a normal person is frequently capable of seeing that a decision is going to create problems, if provided with a feature-intensive link to information that that normal person probably already has. In short, this kind of intellectual activity does not require a genius.

So, those respondents provided with contextual information correctly saw decisions as having negative consequences significantly more frequently than those in the basic scenario condition, in accordance with the theoretical considerations advanced above. The provision of simple information, even if already known to the respondent, was shown to have a positive effect on decision making if made available to the respondent in the proximate context of the decision, as suggested by the work of Bransford and Johnson (1973), Kintsch (1979, 1994), and by the G/FI considerations outlined in detail above. Although we as yet have no information on the relative domain specificity of these effects, future research will undoubtedly provide the answer to this question.

These results indicate very strongly that information simply available in long term memory, or for that matter in extrasomatic sources such as books and hard drives, may have very little bearing on decision making if not made immediately available. Just as a book must be opened, or a computer file accessed, to make the information it contains usable, even relatively simple information must be imme-

diately present in the proximate context of a decision situation if it is to be used. In the absence of such information, as seen in this research and in other work (e.g., Dorner, 1996), decisions may lead to outcomes which are useless or worse (see Wertheimer, 1945/1982). The given decision space may be treated in a gestalt manner as defined above, without analysis of relevant features within the decision space, or of relevant features connecting that decision space to its larger context. But if this type of processing can be reframed to be more feature-intensive, through the simple provision of a relevant feature which either "breaks open" the gestalt process or links it to the larger context in which the decision will have its consequences, the decision may be substantially improved. Positive consequences may be maximized, and, perhaps more importantly, catastrophes averted. This type of simple manipulation, which presumably could be readily taught and which has been shown to operate without reference to intelligence level in a population of normal intelligence, may very well increase the elusive quality of insight (Kohler, 1947; Wertheimer, 1945/1982), so necessary for competent, productive human understanding.

Epilogue

As I write these words, the United States is under attack by military or paramilitary forces, the first time in much of the nation's history that any level of significant attack has ever been directed against its domestic resources. The tragic attacks on the World Trade Center and the Pentagon have been followed by an outbreak of biological attacks, using anthrax as a weapon, which have resulted in a number of civilian deaths. The degree to which the two types of attacks are related is not known at the time of writing. Nor is it known precisely who is responsible for either of them.

The people and leadership of the United States are completely unused to the idea that the nation can be attacked in this way, physically on its own territory. A swift response to the attacks on the Trade Center and the Pentagon is currently under way. The bombardment of much of Afghanistan from the air is proceeding at this moment. Large and small nations, of widely varying military capability, are currently polarizing around the issues involved, and in some cases around old feuds based on various aspects of nationalism and religious conflict.

The situation is, to say the least, volatile. What will happen to a great many nations, and to the people who live in them, depends to a historically extraordinary degree on the decisions that will be made in the next months. Thus it may literally be said that the course and outcomes of the developing war depend more upon human cognition, upon good or bad human decision making, than upon any combination of weapons or political machinations. The crucial role of human cognition in these affairs is not, of course, unique to the present crisis. But that does not render that role any less crucial.

What can be done to ensure that these decisions are good ones, now and in future crises? Decision makers must attempt, as far as is in their power, to avoid grounding their decisions in emotion, in mental set, or in cognitive dissonance. These factors are obvious. Complete information, or information that is as complete as pos-

sible, is also an obvious factor. But as we have already seen, information stored in long-term memory is not enough; it must be brought into the immediate given decision space, reframing that space in more feature-intensive terms, to be of any actual use. This is a critical, and central, message of the research discussed in this volume.

Plato refers to the Socratic doctrine of *anamnesis* in several of the Dialogues (the Meno, the Phaedo, the Theatatus, and indirectly in the Phaedrus; Hamilton & Cairns, 1989). The word simply means "recollection," but it carries far more meaning than that. For the early Platonists, *anamnesis* referred to *active* recollection from the "world of the forms," in essence a realm of perfect abstractions. Modern scholarship, like that of the later Platonists, has of course ultimately rejected the concept of the forms; but the concept of *active recollection*, the idea that information must be *actively drawn into a given decision space* to be of use, may be of considerable importance. The work discussed in this book has shown that mental barriers, barriers to the kinds of mental activities that make such active recollection possible, are not really barriers at all, at least within the research frameworks examined. Rather, they owe their existence to different uses of different types of information under different cognitive circumstances. As such, these "barriers" can be readily broken down. Barriers between the cognitive processing capabilities of young and old; between the realms of verbal, auditory, and pictorial representation; between feature-intensive and gestalt processing; between bad decisions and the information which could turn them into good ones—all can be attenuated or eliminated, by means of judicious manipulation of the processing characteristics which are employed in response to any given cognitive task demands. We are now beginning to understand the continua on which different "kinds" of information lie, and the consequent relationships among information types. We are also beginning to understand how to use this knowledge to diminish or to augment the effectiveness of cognitive processing. In view of the rising importance and consequences of the kinds of decisions which are currently being made on the world stage, it is incumbent upon us to learn how to develop methods of augmenting human information processing and decision making as rapidly as possible.

Bibliography

Ahlberg, S., & Sharps, M. J. Bartlett revisited: Reconfiguration of long-term memory in young and older adults. In press, *Journal of Genetic Psychology*.

Arbuckle, T. Y., Cooney, R., Milne, J., & Melchior, A. (1994). Memory for spatial layouts in relation to age and schema typicality. *Psychology and Aging, 9*, 467-480.

Arnheim, R. (1974). "Gestalt misapplied." *Contemporary Psychology, 19*, 570.

Associated Press (2001, September 9). Tourists pet sharks eating a dead whale. *Fresno Bee*, A-11.

Atkinson, R. C., & Schiffrin, R. M. (1968). Human memory: A proposed system and its control processes. In K. W. Spence (Ed)., *The psychology of learning and motivation: Advances in research and theory*, Vol. 2 (pp. 89-195). New York: Academic Press.

Attneave, F., & Arnoult, M. D. (1956). The quantitative study of shape and pattern recognition. *Psychological Bulletin, 53*, 452-471.

Backman, L., & Larsson, M. (1992). Recall of organizable words and objects in adulthood: Influences of instructions, retention interval, and retrieval cues. *Journal of Gerontology: Psychological Sciences, 47*, 273-278.

Baddeley, A. D. (1976). *The psychology of memory*. New York: Harper & Row.

Baddeley, A. D. (1986). *Working memory*. Oxford: Oxford University Press.

Baddeley, A. D. (1990). *Human memory: Theory and practice*. Boston: Allyn & Bacon.

Baddeley, A. D (2001). Is working memory still working? *American Psychologist, 56*, 851-864.

Baddeley, A. D., & Hitch, G. J. (1974). Working memory. In G. Bower (Ed.), *The psychology of learning and motivation* (Vol. VIII, pp. 47-90). New York: Academic Press.

Baddeley, A. D., & Hitch, G. J. (1993). The recency effect: Implicit learning with explicit retrieval? *Memory and Cognition, 21*, 146-155.

Baddeley, A. D., & Hitch, G. J. (1977). Recency re-examined. In S. Dornic (Ed.), *Attention and performance* (Vol. 6, pp. 647-667). Hillsdale, NJ: Erlbaum.

Baddeley, A. D., & Logie, R. H. (1992). Auditory imagery and working memory. In D. Reisberg (Ed.), *Auditory imagery* (pp. 179-198). Hillsdale, NJ: Erlbaum.

Bartlett, F. C. (1932). *Remembering*. Cambridge: Cambridge University Press.

Bazerman, M. H. (1998). *Judgment in managerial decision making* (4th ed.). New York: Wiley.

Bee Nation Briefs (2001, September 9). Shark bites boy on leg. *Fresno Bee*, A-10.

Bell, J. S. (1987). *Speakable and unspeakable in quantum mechanics.* Cambridge: Cambridge University Press.

Berg, C., Hertzog, C., & Hunt, E. (1982). Age differences in the speed of mental rotation. *Developmental Psychology, 18,* 95-107.

Bergman, E. T., & Roediger, H. L. (1999). Can Bartlett's repeated reproduction experiments be replicated? *Memory and Cognition, 27,* 937-947.

Bethell-Fox, C. E., & Shepard, R. N. (1988). Mental rotation: Effects of stimulus complexity and familiarity. *Journal of Experimental Psychology: Human Perception and Performance, 14,* 12-23.

Bigand, E. (1993). Contributions of music to research on human auditory cognition. In S. McAdams & E. Bigand (Eds.), *Thinking in Sound* (pp. 231-277). New York: Oxford University Press.

Birren, J. E. (1974). Translations in gerontology—from lab to life: Psychophysiology and speed of response. *American Psychologist, 29,* 808-815.

Birren, J. E., Riegel, K. E., & Morrison, D. F. (1962). Age differences in response speed as a function of controlled variations of stimulus conditions: Evidence of a general speed factor. *Gerontologia, 6,* 1-18.

Blanchard-Fields, F. (1986). Reasoning in adolescence and adults on social dilemmas varying in emotional saliency: An adult developmental perspective. *Psychology and Aging, 1,* 325-333.

Bower, G. H. (1970). Mental imagery and associative learning. In L. W. Gregg (Ed.), *Cognition in learning and memory* (pp. 51-88). New York: Wiley.

Bower, G. H., Clark, M. C., Lesgold, A. M., & Winzenz, D. (1969). Hierarchical retrieval schemes in retrieval of categorized word lists. *Journal of Verbal Learning and Verbal Behavior, 8,* 323-343.

Bransford, J. D., & Johnson, M. K. (1973). Considerations of some problems of comprehension. In W. G. Chase (Ed.), *Visual information processing* (pp. 383-438). Orlando, FL: Academic Press.

Brown, J. (1958). Some tests of the decay theory of immediate memory. *Quarterly Journal of Experimental Psychology, 10,* 12-21.

Bruce, D., & Papay, J. (1970). Primacy effects in single-trial free recall. *Journal of Verbal Learning and Verbal Behavior, 9,* 473-486.

Burgin, C. (2000). *California and the civil war.* Fort Point, San Francisco: self-published pamphlet.

Camerer, C. F. (1995). Individual decision making. In J.H. Kagel & A.E. Roth (Eds.), *The handbook of experimental economics* (pp. 587-703). Princeton, NJ: Princeton University Press.

Cerella, J. (1985). Information processing rates in the elderly. *Psychological Bulletin, 98,* 67-83.

Cerella, J. (1990). Aging and information-processing rate. In J. E. Birren and K. W. Schaie (Eds.), *Handbook of the psychology of aging* (5th ed.; pp. 201-221). New York: Academic Press.

Cerella, J., Poon, L. W., & Fozard, J. L. (1981). Mental rotation and age reconsidered. *Journal of Gerontology, 36,* 620-624.

Cerella, J., Poon, L. W., & Williams, D. M. (1980). Age and the complexity hypothesis. In L. W. Poon (Ed.), *Aging in the 1980s: Psychological issues* (pp. 332-342). Washington, DC: American Psychological Association.

Chehile, R. A., Anderson, J. E., Krafczek, S. A., & Coley, S. L. (1996). A syntactic complexity effect with visual patterns: Evidence for the syntactic nature of the memory representation. *Journal of Experimental Psychology: Learning, Memory, and Cognition, 22*, 654-669.

Cherry, K. E., & Park, D. C. (1993). Individual difference and contextual variables influence spatial memory in young and older adults. *Psychology and Aging, 8*, 517-526.

Cialdini, R. B. (1988). *Influence: Science and practice* (2nd ed.). Glenview, IL: Scott, Foresman.

Cohen, J. (1988). *Statistical power analysis for the behavioral sciences* (2nd ed.) New York: Academic Press.

Collins, A. M., & Loftus, E.F. (1975). A spreading activation theory of semantic processing. *Psychological Review, 82*, 407-428.

Cooper, L. A. (1975). Mental rotation of random two-dimensional shapes. *Cognitive Psychology, 7*, 20-43.

Cooper, L. A., & Podgorny, P. (1976). Mental transformations and visual comparison processes: Effects of complexity and similarity. *Journal of Experimental Psychology: Human Perception and Performance, 2*, 503-514.

Corballis, M. C. (1966). Rehearsal and decay in immediate recall of visually and aurally presented items. *Canadian Journal of Psychology, 20*, 43-51.

Cowen, R. (1999). Math error equals loss of Mars orbiter. *Science News, 156*, 229.

Craik, F. I. M. (1977). Age differences in human memory. In J. E. Birren & K. W. Schaie (Eds.), *Handbook of the psychology of aging* (pp. 384-420). New York: Van Nostrand Reinhold.

Craik, F. I. M. (1986). A functional account of age differences in memory. In F. Klix & H. Hagendorf (Eds.), *Human memory and cognitive capabilities* (pp. 409-422). Amsterdam: Elsevier.

Craik, F. I. M. (1994). Memory changes in normal aging. *Current Directions in Psychological Science, 3*, 155-158.

Craik, F. I. M., & Jennings, J. M. (1992). Human memory. In F. I. M. Craik and T. A. Salthouse (Eds.), *The handbook of aging and cognition* (pp. 51-110). Hillsdale, N.J.: Erlbaum.

Craik, F. I. M., & Lockhart, R. S. (1972). Levels of processing: A framework for memory research. *Journal of Verbal Learning and Verbal Behavior, 11*, 671-684.

Craik, F. I. M., & McDowd, J. M. (1987). Age difference in recall and recognition. *Journal of Experimental Psychology: Learning, Memory and Cognition, 13*, 474-479.

Crowder, R. G. (1993). Auditory memory. In S. McAdams & E. Bigand (Eds.), *Thinking in sound* (pp. 113-145). New York: Oxford University Press.

Crowder, R. G. (1976). *Principles of learning and memory*. Hillsdale, NJ: Erlbaum.

Crowder, R. G., & Morton, J. (1969). Precategorical acoustic storage (PAS). *Perception & Psychophysics, 5*, 365-373.

D'Agostino, P. R. (1969). The blocked-random effect in recall and recognition. *Journal of Verbal Learning and Verbal Behavior, 11*, 671-684.

Denney, N. W. (1989). Everyday problem solving: Methodological issues, research findings, and a model. In L. W. Poon, D. C. Rubin, & B. Wilson (Eds.), *Everyday cognition in adulthood and late life* (pp. 330-351). Cambridge: Cambridge University Press.

Denney, N. W. (1990). Adult age differences in traditional and practical problem solving. In E. A. Lovelace (Ed.), *Aging and cognition: Mental process, self awareness and interventions* (pp. 329-349). Amsterdam: Elsevier.

Dorner, D. (1996). *The logic of failure: Why things go wrong and what we can do to make them right*. New York: Metropolitan Books.

Dror, I. E., & Kosslyn, S. M. (1994). Mental imagery and aging. *Psychology and Aging, 9*, 90-102.

Duchek, J. M. (1984). Encoding and retrieval differences between young and old: The impact of attentional capacity usage. *Developmental Psychology, 20*, 1173-1180.

Dyer, G. (1985). *War*. New York: Crown.

Ehrenfels, C. von (1890). Über Gestaltqualitaten. *Vierteljahresschrift der wissenschaftlichen Philosophie, 14*, 249-292.

Einstein, G. O., & Hunt, R. R. (1980). Levels of processing and organization: Additive effects of individual-item and relational processing. *Journal of Experimental Psychology: Human Learning and Memory, 6*, 588-598.

Festinger, L. (1957). *A theory of cognitive dissonance*. Stanford, CA: Stanford University Press.

Fischler, I., Rundus, D., & Atkinson, R. C. (1970). Effects of overt rehearsal procedures on free recall. *Psychonomic Science, 19*, 249-250.

Folk, M. D., & Luce, R. D. (1987). Effects of stimulus complexity on mental rotation rate of polygons. *Journal of Experimental Psychology: Human Perception and Performance, 13*, 395-404.

Freedman, J. L., & Fraser, S. C. (1966). Compliance without pressure: The foot-in-the-door technique. *Journal of Personality and Social Psychology, 4*, 195-202.

Garnham, A., & Oakhill, J. (1994). *Thinking and reasoning*. Oxford, UK: Blackwell.

Gauld, A., & Stephenson, G. M. (1967). Some experiments related to Barlett's theory of remembering. *British Journal of Psychology, 58*, 39-49.

Gauvain, M. (1993). The development of spatial thinking in everyday activity. *Developmental Review, 13*, 92-121.

Gaylord, S. A., & Marsh, G. R. (1975). Age differences in the speed of a spatial cognitive process. *Journal of Gerontology, 30*, 674-678.

Gilovich, T. (1992). *How we know what isn't so*. New York: Free Press.

Glenberg, A. M., Meyer, M., & Lindem, K. (1987). Mental models contribute to foregrounding during text comprehension. *Journal of Memory and Language, 26*, 69-83.

Gollin, E. S., & Sharps, M. J. (1988). Facilitation of categorical blocking depends on stimulus type. *Memory and Cognition, 16*, 539-544.

Greeno, J. G. (1978). Natures of problem solving abilities. In W.K. Estes (Ed.), *Handbook of learning and cognitive processes* (Vol. 5). Hillsdale, NJ: Lawrence Erlbaum.

Grisso, T. (1986). *Evaluating competencies: Forensic assessments and instruments*. New York: Plenum.

Halpern, A. R. (1992). Musical aspects of auditory imagery. In D. Reisberg, (Ed.), *Auditory imagery* (pp. 1-28). Hillsdale, NJ: Lawrence Erlbaum Associates.

Hamilton, E., & Cairns, H. (1989). *The collected dialogues of Plato*. Princeton: Princeton University Press.

Haviland, S.E., & Clark, H.H. (1974). What's new? Acquiring new information as a process of comprehension. *Journal of Verbal Learning and Verbal Behavior*, 13, 512-521.

Henle, M. (1978). Gestalt psychology and gestalt therapy. *Journal of the History of the Behavioral Sciences*, 14, 23-32.

Herman, J. F., & Bruce, P. R. (1983). Adults' mental rotation of spatial information: Effects of age, sex, and cerebral laterality. *Experimental Aging Research, 9*, 83-85.

Hertzog, C., Vernon, M. C., & Rypma, B. (1993). Age differences in mental rotation task performance: The influence of speed/accuracy tradeoffs. *Journal of Gerontology: Psychological Sciences, 48*, P150-P156.

Horowitz, I. L. (2001). Personal communication, 27 December.

Hubbard, T. L., & Stoeckig, K. (1992). The representation of pitch in musical images. In D. Reisberg (Ed.), *Auditory imagery* (pp. 179-198). Hillsdale, NJ: Lawrence Erlbaum Associates.

Humphreys, G. W., & Bruce, V. (1989). *Visual cognition*. Hillsdale, N.J.: Erlbaum.

Hunt, R. R., & Einstein, G. O. (1981). Relational and item-specific information in memory. *Journal of Verbal Learning and Verbal Behavior*, 20, 497-514.

Intons-Peterson, M. J. (1992). Components of auditory imagery. In D. Reisberg (Ed.), *Auditory Imagery* (pp. 45-72). Hillsdale, NJ: Erlbaum.

Jolicoeur, P., Regehr, S., Smith, L., & Smith, G. (1985). Mental rotation of representations of two-dimensional and three-dimensional objects. *Canadian Journal of Psychology, 39*, 100-129.

Kahneman, D., & Tversky, A. (1972). Subjective probability: A judgement of representativeness. *Cognitive Psychology, 3*, pp. 430-454.

Kahneman, D., & Tversky, A. (1979). Prospect theory: An analysis of decision making under risk. *Econometrica, 47*, pp. 263-91.

Kaufman, A. S., & Kaufman N. L. (1990). *Kaufman Brief Intelligence Test Manual*. Circle Pines, MN: American Guidance Service.

Keegan, J. (1998). *The first world war*. New York: Vintage.

Kieras, D. E. (1978). Good and bad structure in simple paragraphs: Effects on apparent theme, reading time, and recall. *Journal of Verbal Learning and Verbal Behavior, 17*, 13-28.

King, C. (1997). Quantum mechanics, chaos and the conscious brain. *Journal of Mind and Behavior, 18*, 155-170.

Kintsch, W. (1979). On modeling comprehension. *Educational Psychologist, 14*, 3-14.

Kintsch, W. (1994). Text comprehension, memory, and learning. *American Psychologist, 49*, 294-303.

Kirkpatrick, E. A. (1894). An experimental study of memory. *Psychological Review, 1*, 602-609.

Koffka, K. (1935). *Principles of Gestalt psychology*. New York: Harcourt, Brace.

Köhler, W. (1925). *The mentality of apes*. New York: Harcourt, Brace.

Köhler, W. (1947). *Gestalt psychology*. New York: Mentor.

Kosslyn, S. M. (1973). Scanning visual images: Some structural implications. *Perception and Psychophysics, 14*, 90-94.

Kosslyn, S. M. (1980). *Image and mind*. Cambridge, MA: Harvard University Press.

Kosslyn, S. M. (1994). *Image and brain*. Cambridge, MA: MIT Press.

Kosslyn, S. M., Ball, T. M., & Reiser, B. J. (1978). Visual images preserve metric spatial information: Evidence from studies of image scanning. *Journal of Experimental Psychology: Human Perception and Performance, 4*, 47-60.

Lakoff, G. (1987). *Women, fire, and dangerous things*. Chicago: University of Chicago Press.

Laughery, K. R., & Pinkus, A. L. (1966). Short-term memory: Effects of acoustic similarity, presentation rate and presentation mode. *Psychonomic Science, 6*, 285-286.

Lawton, M. P. (1982). Competence, environmental press, and adaptation of older people. In M. P. Lawton, P. Windley, & T. Byerts (Eds.), *Aging and the environment: Theoretical approaches* (pp. 33-59). New York: Springer.

Lesgold, A. M., Roth, S. F., & Curtis, M. E. (1979). Foregrounding effects in discourse comprehension. *Journal of Verbal Learning and Verbal Behavior, 18*, 291-308.

Light, L. L. (1990). Interactions between memory and language in old age. In J. E. Birren & K. W. Schaie (Eds.), *Handbook of the psychology of aging* (3rd ed., pp. 275-290). New York: Academic Press.

Light, L. L., & Zelinski, E. M. (1983). Memory for spatial information in young and old adults. *Developmental Psychology, 19*, 901-906.

Logie, R. H. (1989). Characteristics of visual short-term memory. *European Journal of Cognitive Psychology*, 1, 275-284.

Logie, R. H. (1991). Visuo-spatial short-term memory: Visual working memory or visual buffer? In C. Cornoldi & M. McDaniel (Eds.), *Imagery and cognition* (pp. 77-102). New York: Springer-Verlag.

Loftus, E. F. (1975). Leading questions and the eyewitness report. *Cognitive Psychology, 7*, 560-572.

Lorsbach, T. C., & Simpson, G. B. (1988). Dual task performance as a function of adult age and task complexity. *Psychology and Aging, 3*, 210-212.

Luchins, A. (1942). Mechanization in problem solving: The effect of einstellung. *Psychological Monographs, 54* (issue 6).

Madigan, S. A. (1971). Modality and recall order interactions in short-term memory for serial order. *Journal of Experimental Psychology, 87*, 294-296.

Manucy, A. (1949/1985). *Artillery through the ages*. Washington, DC: National Park Service.

Matthiessen, P. (1987). *Wildlife in America*. New York: Viking.

Mayr, E. (1982). The growth of biological thought. Cambridge MA: Harvard University Press.

McAdams, S. (1993). Recognition of sound sources and events. In S. McAdams & E. Bigand (Eds.), *Thinking in sound* (pp. 146-198). New York: Oxford University Press.

McAdams, S., & Bigand, E. (1993). Introduction to auditory cognition. In S. McAdams & E. Bigand (Eds.), *Thinking in sound* (pp. 1-9). New York: Oxford University Press.

McConnell, J.V . (1962). Memory transfer through cannibalism in planarians. *Journal of Neuropsychiatry* (Suppl.), 42-48.

McConnell, J. V. (1964). Cannibalism and memory in flatworms. *New Scientist, 21*, 465-468.

McCormack, P. D. (1982). Coding of spatial information by young and elderly adults. *Journal of Gerontology, 37*, 80-86.

McDowd, J. M., & Craik, F. I. M. (1988). Effects of aging and task difficulty on divided attention performance. *Journal of Experimental Psychology: Human Perception and Performance, 14*, 267-280.

McKay, D. G., & Abrams, L. (1996). Language, memory and aging: Distributed deficits and the structure of new-versus-old connections. In J. E. Birren & K. W. Schaie (Eds)., *Handbook of the psychology of aging* (4th ed., pp. 251-265). New York: Academic Press.

Medin, D. L., & Bazerman, M. H. (1999). Broadening behavioral decision research: Multiple levels of cognitive processing. *Psychonomic Bulletin & Review, 6(4)*, 533-546.

Miller, G. A. (1956). The magical number seven, plus or minus two: Some limits on our capacity for processing information. *Psychological Review, 63*, 81-97.

Murray, D. J., & Roberts, B. (1968). Visual and auditory presentation, presentation rate and short-term memory in children. *British Journal of Psychology, 59*, 119-125.

National Park Service (2000). *Fort Point: Official Map and Guide*. Washington, DC: National Park Service.

Nebes, R. D. (1990). Semantic memory function and dysfunction in Alzheimer's disease. In T. Hess (Ed.), *Aging and cognition: Knowledge organization and utilization* (pp. 265-296). Amsterdam: North-Holland.

Norman, D. A., & Shallice, T. (1986). Attention to action: Willed and automatic control of behaviour. In R. J. Davidson, G. E. Schwarts, & D. Sharpiro (Eds.), *Consciousness and self-regulation: Advances in research and theory* (Vol. 4, pp. 1-18). New York: Plenum.

O'Keefe, J., & Nadel, L. (1978). *The hippocampus as a cognitive map*. Oxford: Oxford University Press.

Paivio, A. (1966). Latency of verbal associations and imagery to noun stimuli as a function of abstractness and generality. *Canadian Journal of Psychology, 20*, 378-387.

Paivio, A. (1971). *Imagery and verbal processes*. New York: Holt, Rinehart, and Winston.

Paivio, A. (1975). Perceptual comparisons through the mind's eye. *Memory and Cognition, 3*, 635-647.

Paivio, A. (1986). *Mental representations: A dual-coding approach*. New York: Oxford University Press.

Paivio, A. (1990). *Mental representations: A dual-coding approach.* Oxford: Oxford University Press.

Paivio, A., & Csapo, K. (1969). Concrete-image and verbal memory codes. *Journal of Experimental Psychology, 80,* 279-285.

Paivio, A., & Csapo, K. (1973). Picture superiority in free recall: Imagery or dual coding? *Cognitive Psychology, 5,* 176-206.

Paivio, A., & Yuille, J. C. (1967). Mediation instructions and word attributes in paired-associate learning. *Psychonomic Science, 8,* 65-66.

Paivio, A., & Yuille, J. C. (1969). Changes in associative strategies and paired-associate learning over trials as a function of word imagery and type of learning set. *Journal of Experimental Psychology, 79,* 458-463.

Park, D. C. (1992). Applied cognitive aging research. In F. I. M. Craik & T. A. Salthouse (Eds.), *Handbook of cognition and aging.* (pp. 449-493). Hillsdale, NJ: Erlbaum.

Park, D. C., Cherry, K. E., Smith, A. D., & Lafronza, V. N. (1990). Effects of distinctive context on memory for objects and their locations in young and older adults. *Psychology and Aging, 5,* 250-255.

Payne, J. W. (1973). Alternative approaches to decision making under risk: Moments versus risk dimensions. *Psychological Bulletin, 80,* 439-453.

Payne, J. W. (1982). Contingent decision behavior. *Psychological Bulletin, 92,* 382-402.

Penney, C. G. (1975). Modality effects in short-term verbal memory. *Psychological Bulletin, 82,* 68-84.

Penney, C. G. (1989). Modality effects and the structure of short-term verbal memory. *Memory and Cognition, 17,* 398-422.

Penrose, R. (1989). *The emperor's new mind.* New York: Penguin Books.

Peterson, L. R., & Peterson, M. J. (1959). Short-term retention of individual verbal items. *Journal of Experimental Psychology, 58,* 193-198.

Pezdek, K. (1983). Memory for items and their spatial locations by young and elderly adults. *Developmental Psychology, 19,* 895-900.

Phillips, W. A., & Christie, D. F. M. (1977). Components of visual memory. *Quarterly Journal of Experimental Psychology, 29,* 117-133.

Puglisi, J. T., & Morell, R. W. (1986). Age-related slowing in mental rotation of three-dimensional objects. *Experimental Aging Research, 12,* 217-220.

Pylyshyn, Z. W. (1973). What the mind's eye tells the mind's brain: A critique of mental imagery. *Psychological Bulletin, 80,* 1-24.

Reason, J. (1984). Absent-mindedness and cognitive control. In J. E. Harris & P. E. Morris (Eds.), *Everyday memory, actions and absent-mindedness* (pp. 113-132). London: Academic Press.

Reese, H. W., & Rodeheaver, D. (1985). Problem solving and complex decision making. In J.E. Birren & K.W. Schaie (Eds.), *Handbook of the psychology of aging* (2nd ed., pp. 474-499). New York: Van Nostrand Reinhold.

Reisberg, D. (Ed., 1992). *Auditory imagery.* Hillsdale, NJ: Lawrence Erlbaum Associates.

Rilling, M. (1996). The mystery of the vanished citations. *American Psychologist, 51,* 589-598.

Roediger, H. L., Wheeler, M. A., & Rajaram, S. (1993). Remembering, knowing, and reconstructing the past. In D. L. Medin (ed.), *The psychology of learning and motivation: Advances in research and theory* (Vol. 30, pp. 97-134.) New York: Academic Press.

Rose, R. G. (1976). Verbal processing of visual stimuli. *Journal of General Psychology, 94,* 233-242.

Routh, D. A. (1971). Independence of the modality effect and amount of silent rehearsal in immediate serial recall. *Journal of Verbal Learning and Verbal Behavior, 10,* 213-218.

Rundus, D. (1971). Analysis of rehearsal processes in free recall. *Journal of Experimental Psychology, 89,* 63-77.

Salthouse, T. A. (1982). *Adult cognition: An experimental psychology of human aging.* New York: Springer-Verlag.

Salthouse, T. A. (1985). Speed of behavior and its implications for cognition. In J. E. Birren and K. W. Schaie (Eds.), *Handbook of the psychology of aging* (2nd ed., pp. 400-426). New York: Van Nostrand Reinhold.

Salthouse, T. A. (1988). Effects of aging on verbal abilities: Examination of the psychometric literature. In L. L. Light & D. M. Burke (Eds.), *Language, memory and aging* (pp. 17-35). New York: Cambridge University Press.

Salthouse, T. A. (1992). Reasoning and spatial abilities. In F. I. M. Craik and T. A. Salthouse (Eds.), *The handbook of aging and cognition* (pp. 167-212). Hillsdale, N.J.: Erlbaum.

Salthouse, T. A. (1994a). The aging of working memory. *Neuropsychology, 8,* 535-543.

Salthouse, T. A. (1994b). The nature of the influence of speed on adult age differences in cognition. *Developmental Psychology, 30,* 240-259.

Salthouse, T. A. (1995). Differential age-related influences on memory for verbal-symbolic information and visual-spatial information? *Journal of Gerontology: Psychological Sciences, 50B,* P93-201.

Satinover, J. (2001). *The quantum brain.* New York: Wiley.

Shallice, T. (1982). Specific impairments of planning. *Philosophical Transactions of the Royal Society, London, Series B, 298,* 199-209.

Sharps, M. J. (1990). A developmental approach to visual cognition in the elderly. In T. Hess (Ed.), *Aging and cognition: Knowledge organization and utilization* (pp. 297-341). North-Holland: Elsevier Science Publishers.

Sharps, M. J. (1991). Spatial memory in young and elderly adults: Category structure of stimulus sets. *Psychology and Aging, 6,* 309-312.

Sharps, M.J. (1993). Gestalt laws of perceptual and cognitive organization. *Magill's Survey of Social Science: Psychology* (pp. 1082-1087). Pasadena, CA: Salem Press.

Sharps, M. J. (1997). Category superiority effects in young and elderly adults. *Journal of Genetic Psychology, 158,* 165-171.

Sharps, M. J. (1998). Age-related change in visual information processing: Toward a unified theory of aging and visual memory. *Current Psychology, 16,* 284-307.

Sharps, M. J., & Antonelli, J. R. S. (1997). Visual and semantic support for paired-associates recall in young and older adults. *Journal of Genetic Psychology, 158,* 347-355.

Sharps, M.J. Foster, B.T., Martin, S.S., & Nunes, M.A. (1999). Spatial and relational frameworks for free recall in young and older adults. *Current Psychology, 18*, 241-253.

Sharps, M. J., & Gollin, E. S. (1986, April). *Enhancement of memory by categorical blocking varies with stimulus type.* Paper presented at the annual meeting of the Rocky Mountain Psychological Association, Denver, CO.

Sharps, M. J., & Gollin, E. S. (1987a). Speed and accuracy of mental image rotation in young and elderly adults. *Journal of Gerontology, 42*, 342-344.

Sharps, M. J., & Gollin, E. S. (1987b). Memory for object locations in young and elderly adults. *Journal of Gerontology, 42*, 336-341.

Sharps, M. J., & Gollin, E. S. (1988). Aging and free recall for items located in space. *Journal of Gerontology: Psychological Sciences, 43*, P8-P11.

Sharps, M. J., & Martin, S. S. (1996, April). *Spatial memory in young and older adults: Environmental support and contextual influences at encoding and retrieval.* Poster session presented at the biannual meeting of the Cognitive Aging Conference, Atlanta, GA.

Sharps, M. J., & Martin, S. S. (1998). Spatial memory in young and older adults: Environmental support and contextual influences at encoding and retrieval. *Journal of Genetic Psychology, 159*, 5-12.

Sharps, M. J., & Martin, S. S. (2002). "Mindless" decision making as failure of contextual reasoning. *Journal of Psychology, 136*, 272-282.

Sharps, M. J., Martin, S. S., Foster, B., & Handorf, K. (1996, June). *Visuospatial support for long-term free recall in young and older adults.* Poster session presented at the meeting of the American Psychological Society, San Francisco, CA.

Sharps, M. J., Martin, S. S., Nunes, M. A., & Merrill, M. (1999). Relational frameworks for recall in young and older adults. *Current Psychology, 18*, 254-271.

Sharps, M. J., & Nunes, M. A. (2002). Gestalt and feature-intensive processing: Toward a unified model of human information processing. *Current Psychology, 21*, 68-84.

Sharps, M. J., & Pollitt, B. K. (1998). Category superiority effects and the processing of auditory images. *The Journal of General Psychology, 125(2)*, 109-116.

Sharps, M. J., & Price J. L. (1992). Auditory imagery and free recall. *Journal of General Psychology, 119*, 81-87.

Sharps, M. J., & Price-Sharps, J. L. (1996). Visual memory support: An effective mnemonic device for older adults. *The Gerontologist, 36*, 706-708.

Sharps, M. J., Price, J. L, Bence, V. M. (1996). Visual and auditory information as determinants of primacy effects. *Journal of General Psychology, 123*, 123-136.

Sharps, M. J., & Tindall, M. H. (1992). Relational and item-specific information in the determination of "blocking effects." *Memory and Cognition, 20*, 183-191.

Sharps, M. J., & Wertheimer, M. (2000). Gestalt perspectives on cognitive science and on experimental psychology. *Review of General Psychology, 4*, 315-336.

Sharps, M. J., Wilson-Leff, C. A., & Price, J. L. (1995). Relational and item-specific information as determinants of category superiority effects. *Journal of General Psychology, 122*, 271-285.

Shepard, R. N., & Metzler, J. (1971). Mental rotation of three dimensional objects. *Science, 171*, 701-703.

Shepard, S., & Metzler, D. (1988). Mental rotation: Effects of dimensionality of objects and type of task. *Journal of Experimental Psychology: Human Perception and Performance, 14*, 3-11.

Shepherd, G. M. (1994). *Neurobiology* (3rd ed.). New York: Oxford University Press.

Simon, H. A. (1957). *Models of man*. New York: Wiley.

Simonton, D. K. (1990). Creativity and wisdom in aging. In J. E. Birren & K. W. Schaie (Eds.), *Handbook of the psychology of aging* (3rd ed., pp. 320-329). New York: Academic Press.

Smith, A., & Park, D. C. (1990). Adult age differences in memory for picture images. In E. A. Lovelace (Ed.), *Aging and cognition: Mental processes, self awareness and interventions*. North Holland: Elsevier Science Publishers B.V.

Smith, R. K., & Noble, C. E. (1965). Effects of a mnemonic technique applied to verbal learning and memory. *Perceptual and Motor Skills, 21*, 123-134.

Sporer, L. S., Malpass, R. S., & Koehnken, G. (1996). *Psychological issues in eyewitness identification*. Mahwah, NJ: Lawrence Erlbaum Associates.

Tulving, E. (1982). Synergistic ecphory in recall and recognition. *Canadian Journal of Psychology, 36*, 130-147.

Tversky, B. (1973). Encoding processes in recognition and recall. *Cognitive Psychology, 5*, 275-287.

Tversky, A., & Kahneman, D. (1972). Subjective probability: A judgement of representativeness. *Cognitive Psychology, 3*, 430-454.

Tversky, A., & Kahneman, D. (1973). Availability: A heuristic for judging frequency and probability. *Cognitive Psychology, 5*, 207-32.

Tversky, A., & Kahneman, D. (1974). Judgement under uncertainty: Heuristics and biases. *Science, 125*, 1124-31.

Vetter, G., Stadler, M., & Haynes, J. D. (1997). Phase transitions in learning. *Journal of Mind and Behavior, 18*, 335-350.

Waddell, K. J., & Rogoff, B. (1981). Effect of contextual organization on spatial memory of middle-aged and older women. *Developmental Psychology, 17*, 878-885.

Watson, J. B. (1913). Psychology as the behaviorist views it. *Psychological Review, 22*, 333-353.

Watson, J. B. (1924). *Behaviorism*. New York: Norton.

Wertheimer, M. (1910). Musik der Wedda. *Sammelbande der internationalen Musikgesellschaft, 11*, 300-309.

Wertheimer, M. (1912a). Uber das Denken der Naturvolker: I. Zahlen und Zahlgebilde. *Zeitschrift fur Psychologie, 60*, 321-378.

Wertheimer, M. (1912b). Experimentelle Studien uber das Sehen von Bewegung. *Zeitschrift fur Psychologie, 61*, 161-265.

Wertheimer, M. (1945/1982). *Productive thinking* (Rev. ed.) Chicago: University of Chicago Press.

Wheeler, M. A. & Roediger, H. L. (1992). Disparate results of repeated testing: Reconciling Ballard's (1913) and Bartlett's (1932) results. *Psychological Science, 3*, 240-245.

Willis, S. L. (1991). Cognition and everyday competence. *Annual Review of Gerontology and Geriatrics, 11,* 80-109.

Willis, S. L. (1995). Everyday problem solving in the cognitive challenged elderly. In M. Smyer, M.B. Kapp, & K.W. Schaie (Eds.), *The impact of the law on aging* (87-126). New York: Springer.

Willis, S. L. (1996). Everyday problem solving. In J.E. Birren and K.W. Schaie (Eds.), *Handbook of the psychology of aging* (4th ed.; pp. 287-307). New York: Academic Press.

Wilson, J. R., DeFries, J. C., McClearn, G. E., Vandenberg, S. G., Johnson, R. C., & Rashad, M. N. (1975). Cognitive abilities: Use of family data as a control to assess sex and age differences in two ethnic groups. *International Journal of Aging and Human Development, 6,* 261-276.

Wilson, M., & Emmorey, K. (1997). A visuospatial "phonological loop" in working memory: Evidence from American Sign Language. *Memory and Cognition, 25,* 313-320.

Wingfield, A., Lindfield, K. C., & Kahana, M. J. (1998). Adult age differences in the temporal characteristics of category free recall. *Psychology and Aging, 13,* 256-266.

Wixted, J. T., & McDowell, J. J. (1989). Contributions to the functional analysis of single-trial free recall. *Journal of Experimental Psychology: Learning, Memory, & Cognition, 15,* 685-697.

Wundt, W. (1897). *Outlines of psychology.* Leipzig: Engelmann.

Wynn, V. E. & Logie, R. H. (1992). The veracity of long-term memories: Did Bartlett get it right? *Applied Cognitive Psychology, 12,* 1-20.

Yates, F. A. (1966). *The art of memory.* Chicago: University of Chicago Press.

Yuille, J. C., & Steiger, J. H. (1982). Nonholistic processing in mental rotation: Some suggestive evidence. *Perception and Psychophysics, 31,* 201-209.

Index

"absent-mindedness," 8
aging
    category structures and, 41–44
    cognitive asynchrony and, 19–21, 73
    cognitive errors and, 6, 40, 45
    cognitive speed and, 18–19, 20–21, 45, 73
    cognitive superiority effect (CSE) and, 39–40
    cognitive task demand characteristics and, 14, 22, 35
    dual coding and, 73
    environmental support and, 45–46
    memory and, 6–7, 18, 45
    mental rotation and, 23–26
    multistore models of memory and, 11
    nonspatial memory and, 40–45
    reasoning and, 7
    recall and, 7, 22, 29, 30, 31–34, 41–43, 46
    recognition and, 22
    relational information and, 39, 42–44, 46
    representation and, 7
    retrieval and, 21, 42–43
    self-initiated processing and, 21–22, 27–28, 34
    semantic memory/processing and, 21
    semantic processing and, 21
    spatial memory/processing and, 26–35, 38–39
    in the study of cognition, 17–18
    verbal memory/processing and, 6, 18, 25, 41–43, 72–73, 84–86
    visual memory/processing and, 6–7, 18, 25–26, 38–39, 41–44, 45, 72–73, 84–86
    "walls" (functional barriers) and, 2–3, 44–45, 46

anamnesis, 124
Anderson, J. E., 90
Atkinson, R. C., 11
attention levels, 8
Attneave-Arnoult figures, 87, 88
auditory imagery, 49–74
    characteristics, 53–55, 59–61
    cognitive superiority effect (CSE) and, 57–61
    defined, 59
    dual coding and, 55–56, 57
    intermediate character of, 59–61, 61, 64–65, 69
    locality of, 50, 58, 70
    phonological loop processing, 58–59, 61, 82
    primacy effect and, 62–69
    recency effect and, 63–65, 65
    resource sharing and, 57, 60, 68–69
    studies of, 49–50
    verbal-auditory-visual continuum, 93
    working memory and, 54

Baddeley, A. D., 57–58, 63–64, 82
Bartlett, Frederic C., 103–4
behavioral decision research (BDR), 114
behaviorism, 52
Bell, J. S., 77
Birren, J. E., 45
"blended" stimuli, 14
Bower, G. H., 67
brain
    head injuries and understanding of brain function, 75–76
    "kinds" of information in, 84
    lobes in, 50–51, 70–71, 76
    mind distinguished from, 1
Bransford, J. D., 43, 116, 117, 120
Broca's area, 70

category structures, 29–31, 38–39
Cerella, J., 19, 24
Chechile, R. A., 90, 102
Cherry, K. E., 29–30
Christie, D. F. M., 65
cognition
    aging in the study of, 17–18
    architecture of, 10–15
    and manifestations of information
        types, 13
    "walls" (functional barriers) in, 1–
        3, 44–45, 46, 70–71, 116–21
cognitive aging. *See* aging
Cognitive Asynchrony Theory
bases of, 18–19, 45
    cognitive asynchrony in, 19–21, 41,
        45
    and free recall, 32–34
    mental rotation and, 23, 29
    relational importation behavior and,
        94
    semantic memory/processing and, 41
    spatial memory/processing and, 26–
        29
    visual memory/processing and, 40,
        41–44, 73
cognitive errors
    about sharks, 5, 8, 10, 14, 45, 74
    aging and, 6, 40, 45
    in Bartlett's "War of the Ghosts" ex-
        periment, 103–4
    in eyewitness accounts, 6, 8, 14, 45,
        74, 92–93
    Fort Point (San Francisco), 8–10, 14,
        45, 74
    Gestalt processing and, 109
    information processing and, 112–13
    mental images and, 53
    "mindlessness" and, 112
    in NASA Mars mission, 5–6, 8, 10,
        14, 45, 74
cognitive speed
    aging and, 18–19, 20–21, 45, 73
    cognitive task demand characteristics
        and, 20–21
    compensating for loss of, 22–23, 32–
        33
    generalized slowing hypothesis, 18–
        19, 21, 25
    and Gestalt and feature-intensive
        processing (G/FI), 93–96, 97–99
    mental rotation and, 23–25

paired associates and, 29
working memory and, 19
cognitive superiority effect (CSE), 37–
    44, 57–63, 85
cognitive task demand characteristics
    aging and, 14, 22, 35
    cognitive speed and, 20–21
    experiential differences and, 26, 35
    and Gestalt and feature-intensive
        processing (G/FI), 89
    importance of, 14
    information processing results and,
        74
    interchangeability of information
        types, 40, 50–51
    level of verbally accessible detail in
        stimuli, 87
    malleability and mutability of men-
        tal images, 83–84
    and the proximate nature of informa-
        tion, 13–14, 71–74
    representation and, 51
    self-initiated processing, 21–22, 34
    spatial memory/processing and, 27–
        28
    synergy between phonological loop
        and visual-spatial sketchpad, 61,
        82
    verbal-auditory-visual continuum
        and, 100–102
    verbal memory/processing and, 18
    visual memory/processing and, 18
    "walls" (functional barriers) and, 2–
        3, 44–45, 46, 117
Cohen, J., 120
Coley, S. L., 90
contextual reasoning, 113–21
Craik, F. I. M., 21, 40, 45

decision making
    availability *vs.* use of information
        (information isolation), 11, 18,
        45, 69–71, 116–21
    behavioral decision research (BDR),
        114
    enhancing, 3
    factors contributing to bad decisions,
        115
    and Gestalt and feature-intensive
        processing (G/FI), 106–21
    long-term memory and, 116
    problem solving and, 114–16

working memory and, 116
Dorner, D., 115
Dror, I. E., 21, 40
dual coding
    aging and, 73
    basis of mnemonic advantage, 62
    in feature-intensive processing, 88
    Paivio and, 79
    recall and, 55–56, 57, 60

Ehrenfels, C. von, 107–8, 108
Einstein, G. O., 31, 37, 45, 82, 87, 90
Emmorey, K., 58, 61
environmental support
    aging and, 45–46
    free recall performance and, 32
    self-initiated processing and, 19, 21–
        22
    spatial memory performance and,
        27–29
    for visual memory/processing, 41

feature-intensive processing. See Gestalt
    and feature-intensive processing (G/
    FI)
flatworms, memory in, 76–77
form, 107–8
Foster, B. T., 33
functional fixedness, 111

Gestalt and feature-intensive processing
    (G/FI), 87–121
    abstraction in, 91–93, 104–5
    cognitive errors and, 109
    cognitive speed and, 89–90, 93–96,
        97–99
    cognitive task demand characteristics
        and, 89
    contextual reasoning and, 113–21
    as a continuum, 89–91, 99–100
    decision making and, 106–21
    errors in eyewitness accounts and,
        92–93
    flexibility in, 97–98, 99
    form and, 107–8
    functional fixedness and, 111
    Gestalt defined, 88, 109
    Gestalt's importance, 104–5, 106
    habit and, 111
    learning and, 105, 110–12
    mental rotation and, 94–96, 106
    mental set and, 111, 115

"mindlessness" and, 112
    organization in, 107–8
    phi phenomenon and, 108
    practice effects and, 98, 99, 102–3,
        106
    productive thinking and, 108–11
    radix and, 109–11, 113
    reasoning and, 102–6, 114
    reconfiguration and, 92–93, 103–4,
        108
    relational importation behavior and,
        94, 96–97
    syntactic complexity and, 90–91, 102
    text comprehension and, 116
    verbal memory/processing and, 88–
        89, 99, 101
    visual memory/processing and, 88–
        89
Gollin, E. S., 24, 25, 29–30

habit, 111
Hitch, G. J., 63–64
Horowitz, I. L., 112
Hunt, R. R., 31, 37, 45, 82, 87, 90

immediate (primary) memory, character-
    istics, 11
information
    availability vs. use in decision mak-
        ing, 11
    functional analysis of, 77–78
    initial encoding, 73
    nature of, 13–16, 71–72
    proximity to decision space, 116–21
    sources of information processing re-
        sults, 74
    ultimate representation, 73
information processing
    cognitive errors and, 112–13
    divisions in, 70
    Swiss army knife metaphor, 87
    ultimate nature of, 75–84
insight, 121
intelligence, paradox of, 10, 114
item identity, 31–33
item-specific/relational information
    theory
    central tenets, 19
    cognitive superiority effect (CSE)
        and, 37–38, 42–44
    primacy effect and, 63–67
    reification of concepts and, 82

relational importation behavior, 29–35, 72, 85–86, 94, 96–97
relational information defined, 64
representational continuum and, 73
spatial memory/processing and, 30–31
syntactic complexity and, 90–91, 102
verbal memory/processing and, 62–63, 73–74, 78
visual imagery and, 62–63, 78

Johnson, M. K., 43, 116, 117, 120

Kintsch, W., 119, 120
Koffka, K., 108
Köhler, W., 108
Kosslyn, S. M., 21, 40, 52, 54, 79
Krafczek, S. A., 90

Lafronza, V. N., 29–30
Lashley, Karl, 76
learning, 105, 110–12
Light, L. L., 21, 27
long-term memory
    boundary with short-term memory, 11
    decision making and, 116
    functional characteristics, 70
    recency effect and, 63
    "War of the Ghosts" experiments, 103
Luchins, A., 111

Martin, S. S., 33
Mayr, E., 13
McConnell, J. V., 77
memory
    aging and (see aging)
    auditory (see auditory imagery)
    chemical, 77
    divisions based on time, 11
    divisions based on type of stimulus encoded, 12
    environmental support for, 20–21
    in flatworms, 76–77
    immediate (primary), characteristics of, 11
    locality of, 75–78
    long-term (see long-term memory)
    multistore models of, 11, 70
    neurotransmitters and, 77
    nonspatial, aging and, 40–45

pictorial (see visual memory/processing)
quantum concepts and, 77–78
recall (see recall)
recognition, 22, 65
retrieval, 14, 21, 42–43
semantic, 21, 38, 39, 41
short-term, 11, 116
verbal (see verbal memory/processing)
visual (see visual memory/processing)
working (see working memory)
"memory molecules," 76–77
memory traces, 32–33, 82
mental images
    cognitive errors and, 53
    malleability and mutability of, 83–84
    ultimate nature of, 86–87
    See also auditory imagery; visual imagery
mental rotation
    Cognitive Asynchrony Theory and, 23, 29
    and Gestalt and feature-intensive processing (G/FI), 94–96, 106
    rate of rotation, 80–81
    reaction time and, 52–53
    spatial memory/processing and, 23–26
mental set, 111, 115
Metzler, J., 53
Miller, G. A., 41
mind
    brain distinguished from, 1
    nature of, 10–15
    "walls" (functional barriers) in, 1–3, 44–45, 46, 70–71, 116–21
"mindlessness," 112
molecular bifurcation theorem, 77

nonspatial memory, aging and, 40–45
Nunes, M. A., 33

olfaction, 71

Paivio, A., 12, 20, 52, 55, 79, 81, 91
Park, D. C., 29–30, 38
Perls, F., 108
Pezdek, K., 27
phi phenomenon, 108
Phillips, W. A., 65

phonological loop, 58–59, 61, 82
planaria, memory in, 76–77
Poon, L. W., 24
practice effects, 98, 99, 102–3, 106
Price, J. L., 39, 59, 61, 66, 68
primacy effect, 62–69
primary (immediate) memory, character-
    istics, 11

radix, 109–11, 113
reasoning, 7, 102–6, 114
recall
    aging and, 7, 22, 29, 30, 31–34, 41–
        43, 46
    category structures and, 32–33, 41–43
    Cognitive Asynchrony Theory and,
        32–33
    cued recall, 22
    dual coding and, 55–56, 57, 60
    free recall, 22, 31–35, 65–66
    paired associates and, 29
    primacy effect and, 65–66
    rehearsal and, 64
    relational cues in, 32–34
    spatial cues in, 32
    visual imagery and, 56
recency effect, 63–65
recognition, 22, 65
recollection, 124
reconfiguration, 92–93, 103–4, 108
rehearsal, 64
reification of concepts, 81–83
representation
    aging and, 7, 18
    cognitive task demand characteristics
        and, 51
    as a continuum, 73, 79
    and electrochemical activity of the
        brain's neurons, 7
    engrams, 76, 78
    information processing results and, 74
    "memory molecules," 76–77
    and processing, 58
    Swiss army knife metaphor, 87
    synthetic theory of, 74
    task dependencies and, 41
    ultimate nature of, 75–84, 86–87, 102
    unitary electrochemical nature, 70–
        71
    See also Gestalt and feature-intensive
        processing (G/FI)
retrieval, 14, 21, 42–43

Rogoff, B., 27
Rose, R. G., 65

Schiffrin, R. M., 11
self-initiated processing, 19, 21–22,
    27–28, 34
semantic memory/processing, 21, 38,
    39, 41
serial position curve, 63
Shepard, R. N., 52, 53, 54, 79
short-term memory, 11, 116
    See also working memory
slowing. See cognitive speed
Smith, A. D., 29–30
spatial memory/processing, 23–35, 38–
    39, 58
speed. See cognitive speed
Swiss army knife metaphor, 87
synergistic ecphory, 82
syntactic complexity, 90–91, 102

text comprehension, 116
Tulving, E., 82

ultimate-versus-proximate cause model,
    12–13, 71–72

verbal memory/processing
    aging and, 6, 18, 25, 41–43, 72–73,
        84–86
    cognitive superiority effect (CSE)
        and, 37–38, 41–43, 44, 60–61,
        62–63, 85
    cognitive task demand characteristics
        and, 18
    dual coding and, 57
    feature-intensive processing and, 88–
        89, 99, 101
    interchangeability with visual
        memory/processing, 14–15, 40,
        41, 47, 49, 51
    item-specific/relational information
        theory and, 62–63, 73–74, 78
    locality of, 50
    primacy effect and, 66–69, 67
    resource sharing and, 30–31, 40, 55–
        56, 79
    spatial memory and, 29–31
    verbal-auditory-visual continuum,
        93, 100–102
    visual memory/processing compared
        to, 12, 14, 20–21, 79

See also semantic memory/process-
ing
visual imagery
    characteristics, 52–55
    cognitive superiority effect (CSE)
        and, 59–61, 62–63
    complexity and rate of rotation, 80–
        81
    dual coding and, 55–56
    item-specific/relational information
        theory and, 62–63, 78
    primacy effect and, 65, 66–69
    "propositional" nature, 79–80, 81, 84
    recall and, 56
    recency effect and, 63–65, 65
    resource sharing and, 68–69, 79
    ultimate nature of, 78–84
visual memory/processing
    aging and, 6–7, 18, 38–39, 41–44,
        45, 72–73, 84–86
    Cognitive Asynchrony Theory and,
        40, 41–44, 73
    cognitive superiority effect (CSE)
        and, 37–38, 44
    cognitive task demand characteristics
        and, 18
    dual coding and, 55–56
    environmental support for, 41
    feature-intensive processing and, 88–
        89
    interchangeability with verbal
        memory/processing, 14–15, 40,
        47, 49, 51
    locality of, 50
    reconfiguration in, 104

resource sharing and, 30–31, 40, 56,
    57, 60
semantic memory/processing and, 41
spatial memory and, 29–31
verbal-auditory-visual continuum,
    93, 100–102
verbal memory/processing compared
    to, 12, 14, 20–21, 79
visual-spatial sketchpad, 58–59, 61,
    82
working memory and, 58
See also spatial memory/processing

Waddell, K. J., 27
"walls" (functional barriers), 1–3, 44–
    45, 46, 70–71, 116–21
"War of the Ghosts," 103
Watson, J. B., 52, 79
Wernicke's area, 70–71
Wertheimer, Max, 108–11, 117
Williams, D. M., 24
Wilson, M., 58, 61
Wilson-Leff, C. A., 39
working memory
    auditory imagery and, 54
    decision making and, 116
    functional characteristics, 70
    in generalized slowing hypothesis,
        19
    theory of, 58, 82
    See also short-term memory
Wundt, Wilhelm, 52, 78–79, 107

Zelinski, E. M., 27